PSALMS

NUMBERS AND DEUTERONOMY SECTIONS
Psalms 90—150

J. Vernon McGee

THOMAS NELSON PUBLISHERS

Nashville

Published in Nashville, Tennessee, by Thomas Nelson, Inc., and distributed in Canada by Lawson Falle, Ltd., Cambridge, Ontario.

Quotations from *The Numerical Bible: Psalms* by F. W. Grant are used by permission of the publisher, Loizeaux Brothers, Inc., Neptune, New Jersey.

Excerpts from *The Book of Psalms* by Arno C. Gaebelein are used by permission of the publishers, Loizeaux Brothers, Inc., Neptune, New Jersey.

Excerpts from *The New Scofield Reference Bible, King James Version*, copyright © 1967 by Oxford University Press, Inc., are reprinted by permission.

Scripture quotations are from the KING JAMES VERSION of the Bible.

Library of Congress Cataloging-in-Publication Data

McGee, J. Vernon (John Vernon), 1904–1988
   [Thru the Bible with J. Vernon McGee]
   Thru the Bible commentary series / J. Vernon McGee.
     p.   cm.
   Reprint. Originally published: Thru the Bible with J. Vernon McGee. 1975.
   Includes bibliographical references.
   ISBN 0-8407-3270-8
   1. Bible—Commentaries. I. Title.
BS491.2.M37   1991
220.7'7—dc20   90–41340
                                    CIP

Printed in the United States of America
1 2 3 4 5 6 7 — 96 95 94 93 92 91

CONTENTS

PSALMS 90—150

PREFACE

The radio broadcasts of the Thru the Bible Radio five-year program were transcribed, edited, and published first in single-volume paperbacks to accommodate the radio audience.

There has been a minimal amount of further editing for this publication. Therefore, these messages are not the word-for-word recording of the taped messages which went out over the air. The changes were necessary to accommodate a reading audience rather than a listening audience.

These are popular messages, prepared originally for a radio audience. They should not be considered a commentary on the entire Bible in any sense of that term. These messages are devoid of any attempt to present a theological or technical commentary on the Bible. Behind these messages is a great deal of research and study in order to interpret the Bible from a popular rather than from a scholarly (and too-often boring) viewpoint.

We have definitely and deliberately attempted "to put the cookies on the bottom shelf so that the kiddies could get them."

The fact that these messages have been translated into many languages for radio broadcasting and have been received with enthusiasm reveals the need for a simple teaching of the whole Bible for the masses of the world.

I am indebted to many people and to many sources for bringing this volume into existence. I should express my especial thanks to my secretary, Gertrude Cutler, who supervised the editorial work; to Dr. Elliott R. Cole, my associate, who handled all the detailed work with the publishers; and finally, to my wife Ruth for tenaciously encouraging me from the beginning to put my notes and messages into printed form.

Solomon wrote, ". . . of making many books there is no end; and much study is a weariness of the flesh" (Eccl. 12:12). On a sea of books that flood the marketplace, we launch this series of THRU THE BIBLE with the hope that it might draw many to the one Book, *The Bible.*

J. VERNON MCGEE

The Book of
PSALMS

INTRODUCTION

The title in the Hebrew means *Oraises* or *Book of Praises*. The title in the Greek suggests the idea of an instrumental accompaniment. Our title comes from the Greek *psalmos*. It is the book of worship. It is the hymn book of the temple.

Many writers contributed one or more psalms. David, "the sweet psalmist of Israel," has seventy-three psalms assigned to him. (Psalm 2 is ascribed to him in Acts 4:25; Psalm 95 is ascribed to him in Hebrews 4:7.) Also he could be the author of some of the "Orphanic" psalms. He was peculiarly endowed to write these songs from experience as well as a special aptitude. He arranged those in existence in his day for temple use. The other writers are as follows: Moses, 1 (90th); Solomon, 2; Sons of Korah, 11; Asaph, 12; Heman, 1 (88th); Ethan, 1 (89th); Hezekiah, 10; "Orphanic," 39 (David may be the writer of some of these). There are 150 psalms.

Christ (the Messiah) is prominent throughout. The King and the kingdom are the theme songs of the Psalms.

The key word in the Book of Psalms is *Hallelujah*, that is, *Praise the Lord*. This phrase has become a Christian cliché, but it is one that should cause a swelling of great emotion in the soul. Hallelujah, praise the Lord!

Psalms 50 and 150 I consider to be the key psalms. Psalm 50, a psalm of Asaph, probably tells more than any other. Psalm 150 is the hallelujah chorus—the word *hallelujah* occurs thirteen times in its six brief verses. It concludes the Book of Psalms and could be considered the chorus of all other psalms.

The Psalms record deep devotion, intense feeling, exalted emotion, and dark dejection. They play upon the keyboard of the human soul with all the stops pulled out. Very candidly, I feel overwhelmed when I come to this marvelous book. It is located in the very center of God's Word. Psalm 119 is in the very center of the Word of God, and it exalts His Word.

This book has blessed the hearts of multitudes down through the ages. When I have been sick at home, or in the hospital, or when some problem is pressing upon my mind and heart, I find myself always turning to the Psalms. They always bless my heart and life. Apparently down through the ages it has been that way. Ambrose, one of the great saints of the church, said, "The Psalms are the voices of the church." Augustine said, "They are the epitome of the whole Scripture." Martin Luther said, "They are a little book for all saints." John Calvin said, "They are the anatomy of all parts of the soul." I like that.

Someone has said that there are 126 psychological experiences—I don't know how they arrived at that number—but I do know that all of them are recorded in the Book of Psalms. It is the only book which contains every experience of a human being. The Psalms run the psychological gamut. Every thought, every impulse, every emotion that sweeps over the soul is recorded in this book. That is the reason, I suppose, that it always speaks to our hearts and finds a responsive chord wherever we turn.

Hooker said of the Psalms, "They are the choice and flower of all things profitable in other books." Donne put it this way, "The Psalms foretell what I, what any, shall do and suffer and say." Herd called the Psalms, "A hymn book for all time." Watts said, "They are the thousand-voiced heart of the church." The place Psalms have held in the lives of God's people testifies to their universality, although they have a peculiar Jewish application. They express the deep feelings of all believing hearts in all generations.

The Psalms are full of Christ. There is a more complete picture of Him in the Psalms than in the Gospels. The Gospels tell us that He went to the mountain to pray, but the Psalms give us His prayer. The

Gospels tell us that He was crucified, but the Psalms tell us what went on in His own heart during the Crucifixion. The Gospels tell us He went back to heaven, but the Psalms begin where the Gospels leave off and show us Christ seated in heaven.

Christ the Messiah is prominent throughout this book. You will remember that the Lord Jesus, when He appeared after His resurrection to those who were His own, said to them, ". . . These are the words which I spake unto you, while I was yet with you, that all things must be fulfilled, which were written in the law of Moses, and in the prophets, and in the psalms, concerning me" (Luke 24:44). Christ is the subject of the Psalms. I think He is the object of praise in every one of them. I will not be able to locate Him in every one of them, but that does not mean that He is not in each psalm; it only means that Vernon McGee is limited. Although all of them have Christ as the object of worship, some are technically called messianic psalms. These record the birth, life, death, resurrection, glory, priesthood, kingship, and return of Christ. There are sixteen messianic psalms that speak specifically about Christ, but as I have already said, all 150 of them are about Him. The book of Psalms is a hymn book and a HIM book—it is all about Him. As we study it, that fact will become very clear.

In a more restrictive sense, the Psalms deal with Christ belonging to Israel and Israel belonging to Christ. Both themes are connected to the rebellion of man. There is no blessing on this earth until Israel and Christ are brought together. The Psalms are Jewish in expectation and hope. They are songs which were adapted to temple worship. That does not mean, however, that they do not have a spiritual application and interpretation for us today. They certainly do. I probably turn to them more than to any other portion of the Word of God, but we need to be a little more exacting in our interpretation of the Psalms. For example, God is not spoken of as a Father in this book. The saints are not called sons. In the Psalms He is God the Father, not the Father God. The abiding presence of the Holy Spirit and the blessed hope of the New Testament are not in this book. Failure to recognize this has led many people astray in their interpretation of Psalm 2. The reference in this song is not to the rapture of the church but to the second coming of Christ to the earth to establish His kingdom and to reign in Jerusalem.

The imprecatory psalms have caused the most criticism because of their vindictiveness and prayers for judgment. These psalms came from a time of war and from a people who under law were looking for justice and peace on earth. My friend, you cannot have peace without putting down unrighteousness and rebellion. Apparently God intends to do just that, and He makes no apology for it. In His own time He will move in judgment upon this earth. In the New Testament the Christian is told to love his enemies, and it may startle you to read prayers in the Psalms that say some very harsh things about the enemy. But judgment is to bring justice upon this earth. Also there are psalms that anticipate the period when Antichrist will be in power. We have no reasonable basis to dictate how people should act or what they should pray under such circumstances.

Other types of psalms include the penitential, historic, nature, pilgrim, Hallel, missionary, puritan, acrostic, and praise of God's Word. This is a rich section we are coming to. We are going to mine for gold and diamonds here, my friend.

The Book of Psalms is not arranged in a haphazard sort of way. Some folk seem to think that the Psalms were dropped into a tub, shaken up, then put together with no arrangement. However, it is interesting to note that one psalm will state a principle, then there will follow several psalms that will be explanatory. Psalms 1—8 are an example of this.

The Book of Psalms is arranged in an orderly manner. In fact, it has been noted for years that the Book of Psalms is arranged and corresponds to the Pentateuch of Moses. There are Genesis, Exodus, Leviticus, Numbers, and Deuteronomy sections, as you will see in the outline which follows.

The correspondence between the Psalms and the Pentateuch is easily seen. For instance, in the Genesis section you see the perfect man in a state of blessedness, as in Psalm 1. Next you have the fall and recovery of man in view. Psalm 2 pictures the rebellious man. In Psalm 3 is the perfect man rejected. In Psalm 4 we see the conflict between the seed of the woman and the serpent. In Psalm 5 we find the perfect man in the midst of enemies. Psalm 6 presents the perfect man in the midst of chastisement with the bruising of his heel. In Psalm 7 we see the perfect man in the midst of false witnesses. Finally, in Psalm 8 we see the salvation of man coming through the bruising of the head. In Psalms 9—15 we see the enemy and Antichrist conflict and the final deliverance. Then in Psalms 16—41 we see Christ in the midst of His people sanctifying them to God. All of this will be seen as we go through the Book of Psalms.

Spurgeon said, "The Book of Psalms instructs us in the use of wings as well as words. It sets us both mounting and singing." This is the book that may make a skylark out of you instead of some other kind of a bird. This book has been called the epitome and analogy of the soul. It has also been designated as the garden of the Scriptures. Out of 219 quotations of the Old Testament in the New Testament, 116 of them are from the Psalms. You will see 150 spiritual songs which undoubtedly at one time were all set to music. This is a book which ought to make our hearts sing.

OUTLINE

I. **Genesis Section, Psalms 1—41**
Man seen in a state of blessedness, fall, and recovery (Man in View)
   A. Perfect Man (Last Adam), Psalm 1
   B. Rebellious Man, Psalm 2
   C. Perfect Man Rejected, Psalm 3
   D. Conflict between Seed of Woman and Serpent, Psalm 4
   E. Perfect Man in Midst of Enemies, Psalm 5
   F. Perfect Man in Midst of Chastisement (Bruising Heel), Psalm 6
   G. Perfect Man in Midst of False Witnesses, Psalm 7
   H. Repair of Man Comes through Man (Bruising Head), Psalm 8
   I. Enemy and Antichrist Conflict; Final Deliverance, Psalms 9—15
   J. Christ in Midst of His People Sanctifying Them to God, Psalms 16—41

II. **Exodus Section, Psalms 42—72**
Ruin and Redemption (Israel in View)
   A. Israel's Ruin, Psalms 42—49
   B. Israel's Redeemer, Psalms 50—60
   C. Israel's Redemption, Psalms 61—72

III. **Leviticus Section, Psalms 73—89**
Darkness and dawn (Sanctuary in View)
Tabernacle, temple, house, assembly and congregation in almost every psalm.

IV. **Numbers Section, Psalms 90—106**
Peril and protection (Earth in View)

V. **Deuteronomy Section, Psalms 107—150**
Perfection and praise of the Word of God

NUMBERS SECTION

Peril and Protection (Earth in view)
Psalms 90—106

This begins the fourth section, the Book of Numbers in the "Penta-teuch" of the Psalms. It opens with a prayer of Moses. It is the only psalm of Moses that we have. Moses was the first writer of the Bible, and you would naturally think that his psalm would be the first one. If you or I had arranged the Psalms, we probably would have placed it at the very beginning. But we did not do the arranging, and I am of the opinion that God supervised even the arrangement because Psalm 90 falls into place in such a wonderful way.

The Book of Numbers records the great tragedy of a generation dying in the wilderness, never reaching the goal, which was the Promised Land. How appropriate it is to begin this Numbers section with Psalm 90, the prayer of Moses.

PSALM 90

THEME: The prayer of Moses

The setting for this psalm is out there on the desert during Israel's wanderings. You recall that when the people of Israel came from the bondage of Egypt, they were led first to Mount Sinai where God gave them the Law. Then they went up to enter the Promised Land; but, instead of entering it, they turned back to that frightful desert. For thirty-eight years they wandered in the desert—until that generation died. Moses saw a lot of people die—over two million of them—and his psalm is the psalm of death.

To me it is a remarkable psalm. It was Martin Luther who wrote: "Just as Moses acts in teaching the law, so does he in this Psalm. For he preaches death, sin and condemnation, in order that he may alarm the proud who are secure in their sins, and that he may set before their eyes their sin and evil." My friend, that is the teaching of this psalm.

Notice how majestic and sublime it is as it opens:

> LORD, **thou hast been our dwelling place in all generations.**
>
> **Before the mountains were brought forth, or ever thou hadst formed the earth and the world, even from everlasting to everlasting, thou art God [Ps. 90:1–2].**

The word *everlasting* is figurative in the Hebrew. It means "*from the* vanishing point *to* the vanishing point." God is from the vanishing point in the past and reaches to the vanishing point in eternity future. Just as far as you can see, from vanishing point to vanishing point, He is still God. How majestic is this thought! Man is just one of God's creatures, an offspring, as it were. In the Book of Genesis Moses wrote, "So God created man in his own image, in the image of God created he him; male and female created he them" (Gen. 1:27). Then in Genesis 2:7 Moses said, "And the LORD God formed man of the dust of the

ground, and breathed into his nostrils the breath of life; and man became a living soul." This psalm regards man as a created being, not as
an evolved animal. He is a creature in a class by himself. He has a
body that was taken from the ground, a body by which he is going to
earn his living down here by the sweat of his brow until the day comes
when it returns to the dust out of which God created it. That's the
picture of man.

> **Thou turnest man to destruction: and sayest, Return, ye
> children of men [Ps. 90:3].**

God returns man's frail body to the dust, saying, "Go back to where
you came from."

> **For a thousand years in thy sight are but as yesterday
> when it is past, and as a watch in the night [Ps. 90:4].**

Suppose, my friend, you live as long as Methuselah lived—almost a
thousand years—that would be like just a watch in the night. It would
be like the flight of a bird through a lighted room, coming out of the
darkness through one window and going out another window into the
darkness again. Even if you could live one thousand years, you
wouldn't be very much. Life is so brief compared to eternity.

> **Thou carriest them away as with a flood; they are as a
> sleep: in the morning they are like grass which groweth
> up.**

> **In the morning it flourisheth, and groweth up; in the
> evening it is cut down, and withereth [Ps. 90:5–6].**

This is a picture of man. In the wilderness Moses saw over one million
people die. He probably attended more funerals than anyone else.
Man's body was taken from the ground, and Moses saw that body put
back into the ground from which it had come.

　　This leads me to another subject. I have received several letters asking me what I think about cremation. I do not believe in cremation. I

don't mean that God cannot raise up your body if you are cremated, but cremation is not a good testimony for a believer. Many unbelievers in Southern California want to be cremated and have their ashes scattered over the ocean. I knew an undertaker in Pasadena who was a pilot. He told me that many people wanted their ashes scattered over the ocean, and that was one of the services he provided. What is the motive of folk who want to be cremated and their ashes scattered over the ocean? Many of them don't want their bodies resurrected; they think that God will not be able to get their bodies back together again.

Christian friend, you give a testimony when you take your dead loved one who is in Christ and you bury him in the ground. In John 12:24 the Lord Jesus Christ said, "Verily, verily, I say unto you, Except a corn of wheat fall into the ground and die, it abideth alone: but if it die, it bringeth forth much fruit." This is the picture of the Lord's death and resurrection. When you bury your loved one, you are planting that body, expecting his resurrection some day. In the early days the cemetery was called two things: (1) an inn, a place where people sleep for a time, and (2) a field, a place where seed is planted. You do not burn up your seed! When you bury your dead, you are planting seed. Your testimony is that you believe God meant what He said when He promised resurrection, and you are looking forward to being reunited with that loved one some day.

> **Thou hast set our iniquities before thee, our secret sins in the light of thy countenance [Ps. 90:8].**

Dr. Lewis Sperry Chafer used to say that secret sin on earth is open scandal in heaven. The angels are watching you; they see what you do down here.

> **For all our days are passed away in thy wrath: we spend our years as a tale that is told [Ps. 90:9].**

In the Hebrew this verse is figurative: "We spend our years as a moan." We go through life moaning. If you do not know the Savior today and have no hope for eternity, you just don't have anything to live for, do you? You don't have purpose in life or any direction.

> **The days of our years are threescore years and ten; and if by reason of strength they be fourscore years, yet is their strength labour and sorrow; for it is soon cut off, and we fly away [Ps. 90:10].**

Threescore years and ten is seventy years. Fourscore years is eighty years. If you make it to eighty years, you sure are going to have a lot of rheumatism and arthritis. I am finding this to be true already. What a picture this gives of us down here! If you live for eighty years, it is going to be uphill all the way. We talk about coming to the "sunset" of life, but that is when you start going uphill, not downhill. We just pass our days as a moan. It is well to have a future, and that is what the believer has when he puts his faith in Christ.

> **So teach us to number our days, that we may apply our hearts unto wisdom [Ps. 90:12].**

It is Christ who is made unto us wisdom. "But of him are ye in Christ Jesus, who of God is made unto us wisdom, and righteousness, and sanctification, and redemption" (1 Cor. 1:30). If you have Christ, you have wisdom and hope.

> **And let the beauty of the LORD our God be upon us: and establish thou the work of our hands upon us; yea, the work of our hands establish thou it [Ps. 90:17].**

Oh, to do something in this life that will have value in eternity!

My friend, Moses out there in the desert, pausing day after day in the wilderness march to bury someone, got a perspective on life that many of us do not have. What a beautiful and practical psalm this is!

PSALM 91

THEME: Song of life and light

As Psalm 90 was a psalm of death, so Psalm 91 is a psalm of life; it is a messianic psalm, and gives a picture of the Lord Jesus Christ. However it reveals a wonderful place of protection and security for us. It is a psalm that is very popular among God's people, both old and young of all ages. Many have been greatly blessed by it.

Psalm 90 was a picture of the first man, Adam; and in Adam all die. It was a psalm of death. But Psalm 91 is a picture of the Lord from heaven, a truly messianic psalm and a psalm of life.

This is a psalm that was quoted by Satan. It is one he knows very well, as we shall see.

> He that dwelleth in the secret place of the most High shall abide under the shadow of the Almighty.
>
> I will say of the LORD, He is my refuge and my fortress: my God; in him will I trust [Ps. 91:1–2].

This is beautiful language, my friend. "I will say of Jehovah, He is my refuge and my fortress." The One who is depicted for us in these verses is the same Man who was the blessed Man in Psalm 1—the Lord Jesus Christ—the perfect, holy, sinless Man. He *always* dwells in the secret place of the Most High. My problem is that I am there sometimes, but my stay is like it is in motels—only for a night or two at a time.

> Surely he shall deliver thee from the snare of the fowler, and from the noisome pestilence [the pestilence that destroys].
>
> He shall cover thee with his feathers, and under his wings shalt thou trust: his truth shall be thy shield and buckler.

> **Thou shalt not be afraid for the terror by night; nor for the arrow that flieth by day [Ps. 91:3–5].**

A young man in my congregation claimed this verse as his when he went into military service. He felt that it brought him through combat safely.

> **Nor for the pestilence that walketh in darkness; nor for the destruction that wasteth at noonday [Ps. 91:6].**

Another young man took this verse with him when he was in the Navy Air Corps. He was a very fine young man, and he retired as a commander. This was the verse he claimed as his.

> **A thousand shall fall at thy side, and ten thousand at thy right hand; but it shall not come nigh thee.**

> **Only with thine eyes shalt thou behold and see the reward of the wicked [Ps. 91:7–8].**

I believe these verses can be used by God's people, and many times God has made them real to His people; but they actually picture our Lord. I want to give you the statement of Dr. A. C. Gaebelein, a Bible teacher of the past generation. He had this to say about this passage: "Let us think of Himself first of all. There was no sin in Him, and that which is the result of sin, disease and death, had no claim on Him. In every way He was the perfect Man, and because He trusted in God His Father, walked in perfect obedience, the great fowler, Satan, could not catch Him, nor the pestilence of destruction. Covered by His feathers, under His wings, the perfect Man on earth found His constant refuge. He knew no fear; that which befell others could never come nigh unto Him. And His own follow Him in the life of trust and obedience, claiming also the preservation and protection" (*The Book of Psalms*, p. 359). I pause to intrude with this: I think that the two young men I mentioned, who claimed verses from this psalm, had a perfect right to do so, and God made them real in their lives. Dr. Gaebelein continues:

"Yet how true it is 'our body is dead on account of sin.' Fanaticism may make claim to all these statements as having an absolute meaning for the trusting child of God, experience teaches often the opposite. Because we are failing and erring creatures of the dust we need discipline and have to pass through the test of faith. Yet in it all the believer can be in perfect peace, knowing that all is well. 'Though He slay me, yet will I trust' is the summit of true faith and confidence in God" (*The Book of Psalms*, p. 360). This is quite a wonderful statement, is it not?

> Because thou hast made the LORD, which is my refuge, even the most High, thy habitation;
>
> There shall no evil befall thee, neither shall any plague come nigh thy dwelling [Ps. 91:9–10].

This pictures Christ, you see.

> For he shall give his angels charge over thee, to keep thee in all thy ways.
>
> They shall bear thee up in their hands, lest thou dash thy foot against a stone [Ps. 91:11–12].

This is the passage that the Devil quoted, and the interesting thing is that Satan knew this psalm applied to the Lord Jesus. He knew something a lot of theology professors don't know today. During the Lord's temptation, Satan said, "For it is written, He shall give his angels charge over thee, to keep thee." This statement is recorded in Luke 4:10; it seems that the Devil quotes Scripture for his purposes. Well, I don't think he can quote it, but he can misquote it, and in this case that is just what he did. He left out the words, "in all thy ways." The Lord Jesus Christ came to do the Father's will, and that meant to walk in His ways. He would have stepped out of the will of God if He had attempted to make the stones into bread, or if He had accepted the kingdoms of the world from Satan, or if He had cast Himself down from the pinnacle of the temple. To do any of that would have been out of the *way* of God. The promise is: "For he shall give his angels charge over thee, to keep thee in all *thy ways.*"

Now in verse 14 there are two "becauses," and they are very important:

> **Because he hath set his love upon me, therefore will I deliver him: I will set him on high, because he hath known my name.**
>
> **He shall call upon me, and I will answer him: I will be with him in trouble; I will deliver him, and honour him [Ps. 91:14–15].**

You see, the perfect Man went into the jaws of death. He went down into the lowest parts of the earth, which meant death and the grave. Deliverance came on the third day when God raised Christ from the dead and gave Him glory. God says, "I will set him on high." What a picture we have of Christ in this psalm!

PSALM 92

THEME: *Song of praise for the sabbath day*

This psalm bears the inscription: "A Psalm or Song for the sabbath day." It is a song of praise that naturally follows a messianic psalm. It tells of praise and worship and adoration—that's what the sabbath was given for. However, worship in this psalm is connected with an earthly sanctuary and actually looks forward to the day when, once again, an earthly sanctuary will be established in Jerusalem and God's redeemed people will worship there. The worship of believers today is a little bit different. The Lord said to the Samaritan woman, ". . . Woman, believe me, the hour cometh, when ye shall neither in this mountain, nor yet at Jerusalem, worship the Father. . . . But the hour cometh, and now is, when the true worshippers shall worship the Father in spirit and in truth: for the Father seeketh such to worship him" (John 4:21, 23). Believers today are made into a kingdom of priests unto God, not to serve Him in an earthly sanctuary, but to worship Him in spirit and in truth.

The psalm opens on this glorious note:

> **It is a good thing to give thanks unto the LORD, and to sing praises unto thy name, O most High [Ps. 92:1].**

Do you want to do a good thing today? Do you want to do a good turn? All right, give thanks to the Lord right now wherever you are and sing praises to His name.

> **To shew forth thy lovingkindness in the morning, and thy faithfulness every night [Ps. 92:2].**

You can thank Him in the morning; you can thank Him at night for His lovingkindness and faithfulness. I always thank Him in the morning. I must confess that I sometimes forget to thank Him at night, but I always thank Him early in the morning for a new day and for His lovingkindness that has brought me to a new day. At night, when you go to bed, you can thank Him for His *faithfulness* in bringing you through the day. I think it is quite an undertaking to bring Vernon McGee through any day. It is wonderful to have a God who will do that!

A brutish man knoweth not; neither doth a fool understand this [Ps. 92:6].

The New Scofield Reference Bible says, "A stupid man knoweth not, neither doth a fool understand this." They do not know about, nor understand, God's lovingkindness or faithfulness.

This is a millennial psalm which looks forward to the future, when the time of worship will once again be on the sabbath day. I don't worship on the sabbath; I worship on the first day of the week, because my Lord was *dead* on the sabbath day. but He came back from the dead on the first day of the week.

But thou, Lord, art most high for evermore [Ps. 92:8].

"Most high" is a millennial name for our God. This psalm is a great millennial psalm, but some verses look back in retrospect to earthly conditions. Man is pictured as brutish. He does not walk uprightly. He does not look up to God. He thinks he does, but he does not. He actually looks down and grovels in the filth of sin. He is a fool. He lacks good sense. He cannot understand because God says, ". . . [his] foolish heart was darkened" (Rom. 1:21). The brutish man denies God, and he lives like a brute. He lives like an animal—like a pig. Many people live as though God does not exist. They just eat, and sleep, and rest, and play, and work. That's it—that's life for them!

But what a beautiful picture we have brought before us here:

**The righteous shall flourish like the palm tree; he shall
grow like a cedar in Lebanon [Ps. 92:12].**

The palm tree has been an emblem of victory, and the cedar tree de-
notes strength and seriousness. This is a picture of the righteous who
are walking in fellowship with God even today.

PSALM 93

THEME: *Millennial psalm of sheer praise*

This is a brief psalm with only five verses. This little psalm, tucked between psalms 92 and 94, is a song of sheer praise because the King is reigning. It is a millennial kingdom psalm and speaks of the Lord who has come to reign gloriously over the earth.

> The LORD reigneth, he is clothed with majesty; the LORD is clothed with strength, wherewith he hath girded himself: the world also is stablished, that it cannot be moved [Ps. 93:1].

"Jehovah reigneth"—this is the Lord Jesus. He is clothed with majesty. This is a psalm that will really have meaning when He comes to reign on this earth. All rebellious opposition will be broken down, and all those who have opposed God will be dethroned on the earth.

> The floods have lifted up, O LORD, the floods have lifted up their voice; the floods lift up their waves [Ps. 93:3].

The flood tide of sin is over. Satan's head has been crushed.

> The LORD on high is mightier than the noise of many waters, yea, than the mighty waves of the sea.
>
> Thy testimonies are very sure: holiness becometh thine house, O LORD, for ever [Ps. 93:4–5].

What a wonderful time of rejoicing this will be!

PSALM 94

THEME: A call upon God to intervene against the wicked

Psalms 94 to 100 form a series of psalms that tell a consecutive story. These seven glorious psalms are kingdom songs celebrating the reign of the Messiah. They are a revelation of the Lord Jesus Christ and His reign on earth following the time of the Great Tribulation and all the trouble that comes upon man during that period.

Psalm 94 is a call upon God to intervene in righteousness against the wicked. It is a cry from the remnant in the time of trouble preceding the kingdom.

> O LORD God, to whom vengeance belongeth; O God, to whom vengeance belongeth, shew thyself [Ps. 94:1].

"Shew thyself" or "shine forth, O God." Many people say, "O, if the Lord would only come." Well, He is coming, friend; but He is coming on His schedule, not on mine or any man's schedule. Then when He comes, He will take care of all those things that caused us suffering. For the present He simply says, "Take my hand, and walk in faith." Vengeance belongs to the Lord. He will repay. God will take care of things and set them right. There are a lot of things that need to be straightened out; and, when He comes to earth again in power and great glory, He will make things right. In the meantime, we are not to avenge ourselves. Turn those matters over to Him.

> Understand, ye brutish among the people: and ye fools, when will ye be wise?
>
> He that planted the ear, shall he not hear? he that formed the eye, shall he not see? [Ps. 94:8–9].

Once again God is speaking to the stupid and foolish man. God is
Spirit. He does not have ears like we do, but He hears. He does not have
eyes like we do, but He sees. The sinner down here on this earth seems
to think he is getting away with sin. God sees; God hears, and He is
able to keep a record of what man does. My friend, there are only two
places for your sins: either they are on Christ, or they are on you. If
they are on Christ, the judgment is passed; if they are not, you have
only judgment to look forward to in the future. Those who are in
Christ have the glorious prospect of life with Him to look forward to in
the days ahead. My friend, if you have not yet come to Christ, you will
have to stand before God in judgment.

> **When I said, My foot slippeth; thy mercy, O Lord, held
> me up [Ps. 94:18].**

The psalmist says, "I would have slipped, but God held me up."

> **And he shall bring upon them their own iniquity, and
> shall cut them off in their own wickedness; yea, the
> Lord our God shall cut them off [Ps. 94:23].**

The psalm concludes with the confidence that God has heard and will
judge the wicked.

PSALMS 95—99

THEME: Songs of joy

Psalm 95 is just a delightful hymn of praise.

> O come, let us sing unto the LORD: let us make a joyful
> noise to the rock of our salvation.

> Let us come before his presence with thanksgiving, and
> make a joyful noise unto him with psalms.

> For the LORD is a great God, and a great King above all
> gods [Ps. 95:1–3].

Then He is worshiped as the Creator:

> In his hand are the deep places of the earth: the strength
> of the hills is his also.

> The sea is his, and he made it: and his hands formed the
> dry land.

> O come, let us worship and bow down: let us kneel be-
> fore the LORD our maker [Ps. 95:4–6].

Psalm 96 is another wonderful psalm of praise when the Lord Jehovah, who is the Lord Jesus Christ, shall reign over the whole earth.

> O sing unto the LORD a new song: sing unto the LORD, all
> the earth [Ps. 96:1].

We have already seen that this "new song" is the song of redemption.
The Book of Revelation says we will sing it.
Here we have idolatry mentioned:

> For the LORD is great, and greatly to be praised: he is to
> be feared above all gods.
>
> For all the gods of the nations are idols: but the LORD
> made the heavens [Ps. 96:4–5].

Idolatry is referred to here because the Millennium will end all idolatry. There are men today who think themselves wondrously wise by turning to all kinds of religions. May I say to you that the day will come when atheism, deism, polytheism, and all of the cults will be done away with.

> Give unto the LORD, O ye kindreds of the people, give
> unto the LORD glory and strength [Ps. 96:7].

The Lord Jesus Christ will fulfill prophecy, end idolatry, and banish Satan; then all creation will rejoice.

Psalm 97 is similar to Psalm 96 because its message is, "Joy to the world, the Lord is come."

> The LORD reigneth; let the earth rejoice; let the multi-
> tude of isles be glad thereof [Ps. 97:1].

This is not a hymn of Christ's first coming to earth but of His second coming to earth.

> Confounded be all they that serve graven images, that
> boast themselves of idols: worship him, all ye gods [Ps.
> 97:7].

"Gods" should be translated angels—compare Hebrews 1:6—"And again, when he bringeth in the first begotten into the world, he saith, And let all the angels of God worship him."

Psalm 98 is the second stanza of the new song of worship.

> O sing unto the LORD a new song; for he hath done mar-
> velous things: his right hand, and his holy arm, hath
> gotten him the victory [Ps. 98:1].

Psalm 99 is a song to the King whose throne is a throne of grace and mercy.

The LORD reigneth; let the people tremble: he sitteth between the cherubims; let the earth be moved [Ps. 99:1].

This is another great psalm of praise to God, the Mighty One. If you haven't formed the habit of praising God, you should. If you are going to heaven, you had better tune up, because you are going to spend a lot of time praising Him in heaven and the best place to tune up is down here. We are going to come to a psalm that says that the Lord is good—let the redeemed of the Lord say so, whom He hath redeemed from the hand of the enemy. That psalm looks to the future when we will praise Him during the Millennium. It is not the Millennium yet, but there is no reason why *we* should not praise Him today. Do you know why we should praise Him? Because He is wonderful, He is faithful, and His lovingkindness endures forever. He will always be good to me, and He will always be good to you. Doesn't this do something for you?

PSALM 100

THEME: Chorus of the hymn to Him

This psalm is the grand finale of that wonderful little cluster of psalms that began with Psalm 94 and closes with this psalm. In this section we have seen the Lord Jesus Christ as King. Jehovah is King. In Psalm 93 we saw that, "The LORD reigneth, he is clothed with majesty . . ." (Ps. 93:1). This phrase speaks of the future and the time that the Lord will come again to earth. The first time He came to earth He did not come in majesty. He came, as George Macdonald put it, "a little baby thing that made a woman cry." He is coming to earth the next time, as we are told in this psalm, "clothed with majesty." Psalm 94:1 begins, "O LORD God, to whom vengeance belongeth. . . ." When the Lord comes to earth again, He will make things right. We could not do it because we would be vindictive; the Lord will not reign that way. He will vindicate, but He will not be vindictive. Then Psalm 95: "O come, let us sing unto the LORD: let us make a joyful noise to the rock of our salvation." Psalm 96: "O sing unto the LORD a new song: sing unto the LORD, all the earth." Psalm 97: "The LORD reigneth; let the earth rejoice. . . ." Psalm 98: "O sing unto the LORD a new song; for he hath done marvelous things. . . ." Psalm 99: "The LORD reigneth; let the people tremble. . . ."

Now we come to the great doxology, Psalm 100. This is the Hallelujah chorus at the conclusion of this series. It is the glorious finale of this very precious cluster of psalms. Listen to it:

> **Make a joyful noise unto the LORD, all ye lands.**
>
> **Serve the LORD with gladness: come before his presence with singing [Ps. 100:1–2].**

Once again I would emphasize the fact that God does not want you to come before Him to worship with a long face. There are times when we have long faces; problems beset us, temptations overcome us, or we come to God in repentance, asking Him for forgiveness. We cast ourselves upon Him. But none of that is worship. You worship God when you come to *praise* Him. He *wants* you to be happy. At the time of this writing most of the bars have what is called a "happy hour." I wish we had a "happy hour" in church, without the liquid. Let's tune up and get ready to worship the Lord. "Make a joyful noise unto the LORD, all ye lands." That includes everybody. That is universal praise. There is a time coming when the entire world will be able to sing, "Joy to the world, the Lord is come!"

"Serve the Lord with gladness: come before his presence with singing." This is a wonderful psalm of praise—praise Him, worship Him, glorify Him. Now that I am a retired preacher I find myself becoming an expert on telling young pastors how they should conduct their services. There is one criticism I want to make concerning my own ministry, and that is that I did not have enough praise included in the services. We ought to praise God more. We ought to worship God more. We ought to come joyfully into His presence.

This psalm is just like a great doxology. There are many doxologies in the Word of God. Believers can sing the one in Ephesians 1:3: "Blessed be the God and Father of our Lord Jesus Christ, who hath blessed us with all spiritual blessings in heavenly places in Christ." God has been good to us. He has given us *all* spiritual blessings, but some of us do not avail ourselves of them; we are keeping them in cold storage, waiting for a rainy day. Well, it is a rainy day today—regardless of how bright the sun is shining. Start using the blessing God has for you! Here is another wonderful doxology in the first chapter of the Revelation: ". . . Unto him that loved us, and washed us from our sins in his own blood, And hath made us kings and priests unto God and his Father; to him be glory and dominion for ever and ever" (Rev. 1:5–6). My, I don't know about you, but that just carries me into the clouds! The whole world is called upon to shout aloud their praises unto Jehovah and to sing the mighty Hallelujah chorus, because in that day the whole world will know Him.

In this next verse is something quite interesting—the homogenizing of God as the Creator and as the Redeemer.

> **Know ye that the LORD he is God: it is he that hath made
> us, and not we ourselves; we are his people, and the
> sheep of his pasture [Ps. 100:3].**

There are a lot of people who do not know that the Lord is God. Many
Christians are not aware of this fact. In the early Christian church
when the first persecution broke out, the apostles came back to the
church in Jerusalem and reported what was happening. Their report
moved the church to pray, and they began their prayer by saying,
"Lord, thou art God . . ." (Acts 4:24). Someone says, "That is easy to
say." Yes, but the question is, Do you believe it today? There are many
Christians who act as if He is not God.

"It is he that hath made us, and not we ourselves"—God is the Creator. We ought to worship Him because He is the Creator! He made this
universe!

Not only do we worship Him as Creator, but "we are his people,
and the sheep of his pasture." How do you become a sheep? You must
be redeemed. This is a case where the Shepherd died for the sheep; the
sheep did not die for this Shepherd. What sheep are being talked about
in this psalm? The sheep are Israel. The Lord is their Shepherd too.
The Lord Jesus told them that He had "other" sheep that were not part
of the flock of Israel. "I am the good shepherd, and know my sheep,
and am known of mine. As the Father knoweth me, even so know I the
Father: and I lay down my life for the sheep. And other sheep I have,
which are not of this fold: them also I must bring, and they shall hear
my voice; and there shall be one fold, and one shepherd" (John
10:14–16). The Lord is the Shepherd of Israel; He is also my Shepherd
and yours—if we belong to Him.

> **Enter into his gates with thanksgiving, and into his
> courts with praise: be thankful unto him, and bless his
> name [Ps. 100:4].**

This is the way God wants you to come into His presence. Someone
told me the other day that he attended the services of one of the great
churches of the past and had never witnessed a place that was so dead.

Do you know what the problem was? People were not coming to church with praise in their hearts. They did not come to the service with thankfulness in their hearts to God. They did not enter His gates with thanksgiving. If you go to church on Sunday to worship, make sure you go with thanksgiving and praise in your heart. If you fail to do that, you are not going to be very helpful to your church.

> For the LORD is good; his mercy is everlasting; and his
> truth endureth to all generations [Ps. 100:5].

I don't know who you are, or why you are, or where you are, but I do know that God is good to you, and He is good to me. Oh, how good He is!

"His mercy is everlasting." He hasn't run out of it. Perhaps since He extended so much mercy to me, you thought He had exhausted His supply. He hasn't. He has a lot left for you. His mercy is everlasting. Like the flour in the barrel belonging to the widow that Elijah helped—it never runs out.

"His truth endureth to all generations." My, what a great psalm of praise this is!

PSALM 101

THEME: *Song to the King who rules in righteousness and judgment*

This is a Davidic psalm. It begins a little nest of six psalms (101—106) that speak of praise to the King. Guess who is the subject of the hymnbook? It is all about Him again, the Lord Jesus Christ. He is the King of righteousness and peace, and He is going to reign on this earth. This is a psalm that could not fit into David's reign at all, so it must be a prophetic psalm. It looks into the future to the Man whom God told David about—the Man who would be coming in David's line. It wasn't about Solomon or any other in the Davidic line until Jesus was born in Bethlehem, because He was of the house and lineage of David. The Lord Jesus is the Man about whom the psalmist is singing.

> **I will sing of mercy and judgment: unto thee, O Lord, will I sing [Ps. 101:1].**

This psalm begins, as others have done, with singing praises to God. "I will sing of mercy and *justice* [rather than judgment]." Now mercy and justice don't get along together today. It is difficult for man to hold them in balance, but God can do it. And we can sing of mercy and justice, because it is "unto thee, O Lord, will I sing." He is the King of righteousness and He is the King of peace. What a wonderful One is presented here!

> **I will behave myself wisely in a perfect way. O when wilt thou come unto me? I will walk within my house with a perfect heart [Ps. 101:2].**

I don't remember David ever walking like that. The One whom we see here is the Redeemer, the only-begotten of the Father. The King speaks as the Son of Man. Notice that He was the Son of Man on the earth. In

His work as the Redeemer He was the only-begotten of the Father, but He took His place in subjection to God's will. He occupied a lower place while He was on earth, but He took it willingly. We attempt to get a higher place. He took a lower place in order that He might bring us to a higher place. Before His incarnation Christ said, "Then said I, Lo, I come (in the volume of the book it is written of me,) to do thy will, O God" (Heb. 10:7). While our Lord was on earth, He stated that His meat and drink were to do the will of the Father who sent Him, and He did *perfectly* His Father's will. He waited patiently for that hour called "My hour" when He wrought out your salvation and mine. Today He is at God's right hand and is still doing the will of His Father. He is waiting for that hour when the Father will send Him into the world again, because the Father has said, ". . . Sit thou at my right hand, until I make thine enemies thy footstool" (Ps. 110:1). We are told that ". . . when all things shall be subdued unto him, then shall the Son also himself be subject unto him that put all things under him, that God may be all in all" (1 Cor. 15:28). This verse has caused a great deal of discussion. What does it really mean? It means that after He reigns on this earth, subject to the Father, He is going back to His place in the Godhead, a member of the Trinity. But when He is on this earth it is said of Him, ". . . I will declare thy name unto my brethren, in the midst of the church will I sing praise unto thee" (Heb. 2:12).

Now notice how Christ is going to reign—and David never reigned like this:

> **A froward heart shall depart from me: I will not know a wicked person.**

> **Whoso privily slandereth his neighbour, him will I cut off: him that hath an high look and a proud heart will not I suffer.**

> **Mine eyes shall be upon the faithful of the land, that they may dwell with me: he that walketh in a perfect way, he shall serve me.**

> **He that worketh deceit shall not dwell within my house: he that telleth lies shall not tarry in my sight.**

I will early destroy all the wicked of the land; that I may cut off all wicked doers from the city of the LORD [Ps. 101:4–8].

Dr. Gaebelein translates these verses a little more clearly: "A perverse heart shall depart from Me, an evil person I will not recognize. Whosoever slandereth his neighbor, I will destroy; him with a lofty look and proud heart I will not suffer. Mine eyes shall be on the faithful of the land, that they may dwell with Me; He that walketh in a perfect way, he shall serve Me. He that is given to deceit shall not dwell within My house, he that speaketh lies shall not be established in My sight. Morning after morning will I destroy all the wicked of the land; that I may cut off all workers of iniquity from the City of Jehovah" (*The Book of Psalms*, p. 379). This is a picture of Christ's reign here on this earth. During the Millennium you will not be able to take your case to the Supreme Court, for the very simple reason that Christ is the Supreme Court. He is the only One who will judge. The Father has turned over all judgment to His Son, and He will judge everyone every morning. They will have to toe the mark. The Lord is going to be a dictator when He reigns on earth, and everyone will do His will.

Then they will sing a new song to the King who rules in righteousness and judgment.

PSALM 102

THEME: Prayer of trouble and sorrow

This is a messianic psalm that pictures the Lord Jesus in Gethsemane. The writer of this psalm is not mentioned. Since there have been all sorts of guesses as to who wrote it, I will guess that it was David. The inspired inscription of this psalm is "A Prayer of the afflicted, when he is overwhelmed, and poureth out his complaint before the LORD." This psalm pictures the affliction and humiliation of our Lord in the Garden of Gethsemane. As we will soon find, the Holy Spirit has marked out this psalm as messianic in the New Testament.

Hear my prayer, O LORD, and let my cry come unto thee [Ps. 102:1].

Dr. Gaebelein's translation is: "Jehovah, hear My prayer and let My cry come unto Thee!" Here is a case where Jehovah prays to Jehovah! He came in humiliation; yet He was Jehovah manifested in the flesh. In Genesis we find a remarkable statement: "Then the LORD rained upon Sodom and upon Gomorrah brimstone and fire from the LORD out of heaven" (Gen. 19:24). In other words, Jehovah on earth asks Jehovah in heaven to bring down judgment. Dr. Gaebelein adds this comment: "But here in humiliation, facing His great work as the sinbearer, the fellow of Jehovah (Zech. 13:7) cries unto Him 'that was able to save Him out of death.' We have here in prophecy 'the prayers and supplications with strong crying and tears' of Gethsemane (Heb. 5:7)." And He was heard. But we find here that the wrath of the holy and righteous God fell upon Him because He bore your sins and my sins.

What a glorious and wonderful psalm this is!

Now here we see the deepest woe and agony that man can have:

Mine enemies reproach me all the day; and they that are mad against me are sworn against me [Ps. 102:8].

This expresses the depth of despair.

> **Because of thine indignation and thy wrath: for thou
> hast lifted me up, and cast me down [Ps. 102:10].**

The words *indignation* and *wrath* are the strongest terms you can use
in the Hebrew language. The Lord endured this. Why? He did it
". . . for the *joy* that was set before him . . ." (Heb. 12:2).

> **But thou, O Lord, shalt endure for ever; and thy remem-
> brance unto all generations.**

> **Thou shalt arise, and have mercy upon Zion: for the
> time to favour her, yea, the set time, is come [Ps.
> 102:12–13].**

He will have mercy upon Zion! And so it was ". . . for the joy that was
set before him endured the cross, despising the shame . . ." (Heb.
12:2). He died, you see, for the nation Israel. John 11:51 mentions that
it was necessary for one to die for the nation. And Christ did die for
that nation.

And He is going to build Zion again when He appears in His
glory—which will be at His second coming.

> **When the Lord shall build up Zion, he shall appear in
> his glory [Ps. 102:16].**

Our Lord knew that through His sacrificial death Zion would ulti-
mately be redeemed.

> **Of old hast thou laid the foundation of the earth: and the
> heavens are the work of thy hands.**

> **They shall perish, but thou shalt endure: yea, all of
> them shall wax old like a garment; as a vesture shalt
> thou change them, and they shall be changed.**

**But thou art the same, and thy years shall have no end
[Ps. 102:25–27].**

The Holy Spirit quotes this passage in Hebrews 1:10–12, and we
would not have known that Psalm 102 was a messianic psalm if it
hadn't pleased the author of the Bible, the Spirit of God, to reveal the
meaning of this section in the first chapter of Hebrews. Psalm 102
applies to the Lord Jesus Christ. It is His prayer of trouble and sorrow.
This is the King in Gethsemane—His humiliation before His exaltation, as set forth in Hebrews 5:7, which says, "Who in the days of his
flesh, when he had offered up prayers and supplications with strong
crying and tears unto him that was able to save him from death, and
was heard in that he feared." Because He suffered for us, He can sym-
pathize with us. I like to think of Psalm 102 as the psalm of Gethsemane.

PSALM 103

THEME: A great psalm of praise for the tender mercies of God

When Gustavus Adolphus entered Augsburg after his victory at Leipzig, he had this psalm read. It looks forward to a new day; in fact, it looks beyond the Millennium into eternity where it will find the fullness of fulfillment. In the past the nation of Israel turned to this psalm, today the godly Israelite turns to this psalm, and in the future he will also turn to this psalm. Individual believers today find it a real source of strength and light. It is a psalm of thanksgiving for things, and a psalm of praise for a Person—that Person is Christ. I suppose it was sung antiphonally. The psalm begins as a solo and ends in a symphony of universal praise. I have divided the psalm like this: (1) Admonition for the present; (2) Declaration concerning Jehovah; (3) Declaration concerning man; and (4) Proclamation for the future.

ADMONITION FOR THE PRESENT

Psalm 103 begins with an admonition for the present, and notice how personal it is.

> **Bless the LORD, O my soul: and all that is within me, bless his holy name.**
>
> **Bless the LORD, O my soul, and forget not all his benefits [Ps. 103:1–2].**

Twice we are told to bless the Lord, twice in the first two verses. This is a psalm that gets way down where we live; it reveals something to our hearts. The Polychrome Bible translates the first verse, "Bless the LORD, O my soul: and all that is deepest within me, bless his holy name." We are told to praise and glorify the Lord; yet when I read this psalm I recognize that the best I can do just doesn't quite make it. My soul goes out to Him but not like it should. My friend, I want to put up a warning signal. There is a real danger today of going to church, observing the ritual, and parroting pious platitudes. This is the thing God warned His people about in Isaiah 29:13, "Wherefore the Lord said, Forasmuch as this people draw near me with their mouth, and with their lips do honour me, but have removed their heart far from me, and their fear toward me is taught by the precept of men." It is nothing more than lip service. There is no submission to God's Word and His demands. They just follow the precepts of men. We see this in Judaism and Romanism; and it is pretty easy for Protestants to point a finger at them and say, "Look how dead their religion is!" My friend, how dead is your church and your personal worship? Oh, if only my praise could be pure and from the depths of my heart! That is what I long for and what we should all long for. There is a lot of chanting and ritualism today in church. It is easy to say that liberalism rejects all of the great truths of God's Word, but if we simply go to church and mouth these truths, it can also be said of us, "Men worship Me with their lips, but their hearts are far from Me." This psalm says, "*All* that is within me, bless his holy name." The flesh cannot do this. I am going to make a confession to you: I can't worship the Lord like I want to. Do you know why? This old flesh of mine can't rise to that level. It is only by the Holy Spirit that you and I can worship the Lord in spirit and in truth.

Let's not forget "all His benefits." He has been so good to us—how evident this is as we look back over the years.

DECLARATION CONCERNING JEHOVAH

Who forgiveth all thine iniquities; who healeth all thy diseases [Ps. 103:3].

I am of the opinion that this verse speaks of the kingdom age (there are many people who disagree with me), and I am very frank to say that this refers to physical as well as spiritual diseases. God has made it quite clear what He is going to do during the kingdom age. Isaiah

33:24 says, "And the inhabitant shall not say, I am sick: the people that dwell therein shall be forgiven their iniquity." I have been told that many of these "faith healers" emphasize salvation. I don't think they emphasize salvation at all. Instead they put it on the end of their services like a caboose. My friend, there can be no healing until the sins are forgiven. Disease is the result of sin; and, before healing can take place, the sin question must be settled. Christ was delivered for our offenses. He was raised for our justification. Not until we are justified by faith in Christ can we be forgiven. In 1 Peter 2:24 (a quote from Isaiah 53:5) we read, "Who his own self bare our sins in his own body on the tree, that we, being dead to sins, should live unto righteousness: by whose stripes ye were healed." Healed of what? Healed of your sins, my friend. That is the important thing.

> **Who redeemeth thy life from destruction; who crowneth thee with lovingkindness and tender mercies [Ps. 103:4].**

We ought to recognize the fact that many of God's choicest servants have been ill and afflicted and have never been healed in this life. The apostle Paul was one of these. He had a thorn in his flesh. It may have been eye trouble. If anyone should have claimed healing, it seems to me he should have. Fanny Crosby was blind to her dying day. John Milton was blind. What about these people? Do you have the audacity to say that something was wrong with these people because they were not healed? It is wonderful to be healed, but that is not always God's plan. Understand one thing: some of God's choicest servants never experienced healing at all.

> **Who satisfieth thy mouth with good things; so that thy youth is renewed like the eagle's [Ps. 103:5].**

I was very amused one day when I saw a "faith healer" on television. In fact, I was shocked because the picture I had seen of her looked very much like that of a high school girl. What I saw on television was not a high school girl—God had not renewed her youth. That will take place during the Millennium. In fact, I have a new body coming to me. I don't have it yet, but one day in the future it will be mine.

> The LORD executeth righteousness and judgment for all that are oppressed.

> He made known his ways unto Moses, his acts unto the children of Israel [Ps. 103:6–7].

God made known His *ways* to Moses, but all that the children of Israel saw were the miracles. They did not have much understanding. There are many people like them today who recognize certain truths, but they don't enter into the way of God. Oh, how important that is.

> The LORD is merciful and gracious, slow to anger, and plenteous in mercy [Ps. 103:8].

What we need above everything else today is God's mercy.

DECLARATION CONCERNING MAN

> He will not always chide: neither will he keep his anger for ever.

> He hath not dealt with us after our sins; nor rewarded us according to our iniquities [Ps. 103:9–10].

My friend, if God would deal with us according to our sins and according to our iniquities, none of us would be saved.

> For as the heaven is high above the earth, so great is his mercy toward them that fear him [Ps. 103:11].

Oh, how we need his mercy!

> As far as the east is from the west, so far hath he removed our transgressions from us [Ps. 103:12].

The psalmist does not say, "As far as the north is from the south." That is quite a distance; but when you start moving from the east to the west, there is no end. When you start going west, you keep going west. When you go north, you eventually reach a point where you start going south, but when you go west, you never stop going west. That is how far God has removed our transgressions from us!

> **Like as a father pitieth his children, so the LORD pitieth them that fear him [Ps. 103:13].**

God is so good to us, and we do not seem to recognize it.

> **For he knoweth our frame; he remembereth that we are dust [Ps. 103:14].**

Dr. George Gill used to put it like this: "God remembers that we are dust. We forget it, and when dust gets stuck on itself, it is mud." That is a picture of man.

> **As for man, his days are as grass: as a flower of the field, so he flourisheth.**
>
> **For the wind passeth over it, and it is gone; and the place thereof shall know it no more [Ps. 103: 15–16].**

We won't be here on earth very long, friend. Someone said to me the other day, "I notice you are getting a little gray." I replied, "I notice that you are, too." Do you know what God is trying to tell us? When God puts gray in your hair, He is saying, "You are not going to be here much longer." When you get arthritis and you have trouble getting up in the morning, that is a warning from God. He is saying, "You won't be around much longer. You need to get straightened out."

PROCLAMATION FOR THE FUTURE

> **But the mercy of the LORD is from everlasting to everlasting upon them that fear him, and his righteousness unto children's children [Ps. 103:17].**

It is a wonderful thing to look into the future and know that God will always be merciful to us.

> Bless the LORD, all his works in all places of his dominion: bless the LORD, O my soul [Ps. 103:22].

How glorious it will be when all creatures in His dominion will bless Him. This is universal worship when, as Dr. Gaebelein expresses it, "the mighty Hallelujahs will sweep the earth, will sweep the heavens, will come downward and upward, when all creation will join in, when everything which has breath will shout 'Hallelujah.'"

But in the meantime, let's not forget to "bless the LORD, O my soul."

PSALM 104

THEME: Praise to the God of creation

This is a psalm of nature, or as *The New Scofield Reference Bible* puts it, "Praise to the God of creation." It begins:

> **Bless the Lord, O my soul. O Lord my God, thou art very great; thou art clothed with honour and majesty [Ps. 104:1].**

This psalm speaks about the God of creation. It is a hymn to God in nature because He is Creator.

> **Who coverest thyself with light as with a garment: who stretchest out the heavens like a curtain [Ps. 104:2].**

On the first day of creation God said, ". . . Let there be light: and there was light" (Gen. 1:3). The second day of creation is pictured in these words: "Who stretchest out the heavens like a curtain"—just as you would stretch out a tent. In the day this psalm was written, travelers, such as those with a camel caravan, would arrive at their stopping place for the night and stretch out their tents. Well, that is the way God stretched out the heavens. As He did this, He put a layer of water above (and sometimes it comes down pretty fast), and the clouds are His chariots.

> **Who layeth the beams of his chambers in the waters: who maketh the clouds his chariot: who walketh upon the wings of the wind [Ps. 104:3].**

On the second day of creation God said, ". . . Let there be a firmament in the midst of the waters, and let it divide the waters from the waters" (Gen. 1:6).

> Who laid the foundations of the earth, that it should not be removed for ever.
>
> Thou coveredst it with the deep as with a garment: the waters stood above the mountains [Ps. 104:5-6].

On the third day of creation ". . . God said, Let the waters under the heaven be gathered together unto one place, and let the dry land appear: and it was so" (Gen. 1:9). He had put waters above them—the clouds that go over carry quite a bit of water—now He divides the land and the waters.

> At thy rebuke they fled; at the voice of thy thunder they hasted away.
>
> They go up by the mountains; they go down by the valleys unto the place which thou hast founded for them [Ps. 104:7-8].

On the fourth day God did not create the sun and moon; He simply said, ". . . Let there be lights in the firmament of the heaven to divide the day from the night; and let them be for signs, and for seasons, and for days, and years" (Gen. 1:14). The sun and moon are to regulate time here on this earth. We have this in verse 19:

> He appointed the moon for seasons: the sun knoweth his going down [Ps. 104:19].

Ancient people learned that the sun and moon regulated seedtime and harvest on the earth. In the ruins of an Indian building in Arizona are two holes which were made in a wall. For a long time no one could figure out why they were there. They finally discovered that when you could look through both of those holes and see the moon it was time to plant corn. God gave us the moon for seasons—He says so. The sun and the moon move according to schedule. Don't tell me that we are living in a meaningless universe.

What did God create on the fifth day? That was the day animal life appeared.

> So is this great and wide sea, wherein are things creeping innumerable, both small and great beasts.
>
> There go the ships: there is that leviathan, whom thou hast made to play therein [Ps. 104:25–26].

"And God said, Let the waters bring forth abundantly the moving creature that hath life . . ." (Gen. 1:20). It became alive with living creatures and everything that is in the ocean.

Now, what about man?

> Thou sendest forth thy spirit, they are created: and thou renewest the face of the earth [Ps. 104:30].

Man now is going to be put on the earth—his home is ready for him.

> The glory of the LORD shall endure for ever: the LORD shall rejoice in his works [Ps. 104:31].

When His creation was finished, God looked upon it and saw that it was good.

> He looketh on the earth, and it trembleth: he toucheth the hills, and they smoke.
>
> I will sing unto the LORD as long as I live: I will sing praise to my God while I have my being [Ps. 104:32–33].

Man is on the earth, created to praise God. He has been put on earth, and he has an address: he lives at No. 1, Garden of Eden.

> My meditation of him shall be sweet: I will be glad in the LORD [Ps. 104:34].

However—

**Let the sinners be consumed out of the earth, and let the
wicked be no more. Bless thou the LORD, O my soul.
Praise ye the LORD [Ps. 104:35].**

Man has sinned. So what will God do? He is going to remove him from
the earth, my friend. Unless you are willing to turn to Christ, I can
assure you of one thing: this earth will not be your permanent dwell-
ing place. God will remove you to another place, and He has another
address for you.

PSALMS 105 AND 106

THEME: Historic psalms

Psalm 105 is a hymn to God in history from Abraham to Moses. I am confident that it was written by David because the first part of this psalm is the same as 1 Chronicles 16:8–22, which tells about the time David brought the tabernacle into Jerusalem. This psalm is a recitation of Israel's history.

> **O give thanks unto the LORD; call upon his name: make known his deeds among the people.**
>
> **Sing unto him, sing psalms unto him: talk ye of all his wondrous works.**
>
> **Glory ye in his holy name: let the heart of them rejoice that seek the LORD.**
>
> **Seek the LORD, and his strength: seek his face evermore.**
>
> **Remember his marvellous works that he hath done; his wonders, and the judgments of his mouth [Ps. 105:1–5].**

He goes back in history and begins with the descendants of Abraham, and the covenant God made with Abraham, Isaac, and Jacob. Then He follows them through Joseph, down into the land of Egypt.

> **Israel also came into Egypt; and Jacob sojourned in the land of Ham [Ps. 105:23].**

Then when His people were oppressed by the Egyptians—

> **He sent Moses his servant; and Aaron whom he had chosen.**

They shewed his signs among them, and wonders in the land of Ham [Ps. 105:26–27].

Now here is an interesting comment—

Egypt was glad when they departed: for the fear of them fell upon them [Ps. 105:38].

"Egypt was glad when Israel departed"—they certainly were. They were glad to get Israel out of their hair after those plagues. Then God brought His people into the land. The psalmist recites Israel's history as something to sing praise about.

My friend, there is something wrong with you if you cannot look back through your life and find something to thank God for. As the final verse of this psalm says, "Praise ye the LORD."

Psalm 106 is another historic psalm, and a long one; it ends the Numbers section. It follows the children of Israel through the wilderness. It begins:

Praise ye the LORD. O give thanks unto the LORD; for he is good: for his mercy endureth for ever [Ps. 106:1].

This psalm also speaks about the confession of sins.

We have sinned with our fathers, we have committed iniquity, we have done wickedly [Ps. 106:6].

When you look back over your life, you have something to thank God for if you have turned to Jesus Christ as your Savior and asked Him to forgive your sins. You can *thank* God for your salvation. These psalms are marvelous, are they not? This psalm shows us Israel's failure and God's faithfulness. We ought to become saturated with these psalms.

DEUTERONOMY SECTION

Perfection and Praise of the Word of God
Psalms 107—150

Psalm 107 begins the Deuteronomy section of the Book of Psalms. Dr. Gaebelein makes this comment: "The fifth book written by Moses begins with a great retrospect in the plains of Moab, in which inspired Moses reviews God's gracious dealing with His people. They were then facing the land of promise, into which they were soon to enter. In the opening psalm of this Deuteronomy section the remnant of Israel is seen prophetically regathered and about ready to enter the land. They are looking back over their age-long experiences, how He led them, dealt with them, humbled them, preserved and kept them" (*The Book of Psalms*, p. 399).

Believers of all ages have shared experiences such as these in their personal lives, and they are applicable to you and me.

PSALM 107

THEME: God is good

This is a psalm that has been greatly misunderstood. I feel that an excellent commentator like Matthew Henry, who had wonderful things to say about this psalm, missed it because he did not see the prophetic aspect of it. I trust by now that you are seeing the deep meaning in these psalms when they are put in their proper context. It is the song of the wandering Jew when he reenters the Promised Land. Also this psalm has a special meaning for us in our day and has blessed the hearts of saints down through the ages.

This is a psalm I would like to see set to music. It divides itself naturally into four stanzas, and the chorus is repeated three times (vv. 8, 21, and 31).

THE PROVIDENCE OF GOD—HE DIRECTS PILGRIMS

My suggestion would be that this be sung as a tenor solo.

> O give thanks unto the LORD, for he is good: for his mercy endureth for ever.
>
> Let the redeemed of the LORD say so, whom he hath redeemed from the hand of the enemy [Ps. 107:1–2].

We need more "say so" Christians. Let the redeemed of the Lord *say so*. Don't go around complaining and criticizing. If you are a Christian, tell others how good God is. He *is* good, but He doesn't have a good name in the world today. God's reputation is bad—a reputation is what people think about you. God does not have many friends in court among the multitudes of people in the world—no champion, or defender, and few to testify on His behalf. There are few to take the witness stand and say a good word in His behalf. If you doubt that, look around. Consider the pagan and heathen religions. Their conception of God is terrifying. He is pictured as a god that will destroy, not save; a god that is difficult to approach, and takes no personal interest in his creatures, nor does he love them. The average person today lives in a land with a veneer of civilization, a modicum of education, with a little Christian culture smeared on like face cream. To him God is not a Person to be cultivated; He is kept at arm's length. He is not considered a good neighbor, and He is very hard to please. Most people think of God as sort of a policeman, waiting around the corner to catch them in some wrongdoing. A little girl accidentally gave the average conception of God when she recited a Scripture verse and got it a bit confused. She said, "If God be for you, you are up against Him." That is the thinking of many people.

If anyone is going to say that God is good, it will have to be His redeemed ones. *God is good.* That is not an axiom; it is a proposition that is subject to proof. It is not a cliché, nor a slogan; it is not propaganda. It is true.

> And gathered them out of the lands, from the east, and
> from the west, from the north, and from the south [Ps.
> 107:3].

The Lord is gathering people from the east, west, north, and south.
Who are they? God is talking about Israel.

> They wandered in the wilderness in a solitary way; they
> found no city to dwell in.
>
> Hungry and thirsty, their soul fainted in them.
>
> Then they cried unto the LORD in their trouble, and he
> delivered them out of their distresses.
>
> And he led them forth by the right way, that they might
> go to a city of habitation [Ps. 107:4–7].

Remember that Psalm 107 begins the Deuteronomy section of the
Psalms and corresponds to the Book of Deuteronomy, the last book of
the Pentateuch which was written by Moses. This section deals with
the perfection and praise of God's Word. In Deuteronomy 28: 64–65,
God already told the Israelites that they would be scattered because of
their sins: "And the LORD shall scatter thee among all people, from the
one end of the earth even unto the other; and there thou shalt serve
other gods, which neither thou nor thy fathers have known, even wood
and stone. And among these nations shalt thou find no ease, neither
shall the sole of thy foot have rest: but the LORD shall give thee there a
trembling heart, and failing of eyes, and sorrow of mind." This has
been the picture of the Jews down through the ages when they dis-
obeyed God and were out of their land. But God is going to gather
them together once again and make good His promise to establish
them in the land. This is a wonderful picture of the providence of God
in the lives of His people.

It speaks of me also. God reached down in the wilderness of this
world and saved me. He will do the same for you, if He hasn't already
done so. This is a glorious picture of the providence of God in the lives
of His ancient people—God is not through with the nation Israel. In

fact, God is not through with you and He is not through with me. This section has a message for us.

THE PARDON OF GOD—HE DELIVERS PRISONERS

Let's make this a soprano solo. It begins on that high note of praise. In fact, it begins with this wonderful chorus:

> **Oh that men would praise the LORD for his goodness, and for his wonderful works to the children of men! [Ps. 107:8].**

The chorus is at the beginning of this section rather than at the end.

As we move down into this psalm, we will notice that God delivers prisoners, and we will see a picture of a man in prison. It describes Israel in the time of trouble, the Great Tribulation that is coming. If a man is in prison at that time, God will deliver him and bring him back into the land. Think of the multitudes in prison in Germany during World War II, and all of them did not get out. I wonder how many of them thought of this psalm at that time?

> **Such as sit in darkness and in the shadow of death, being bound in affliction and iron [Ps. 107:10].**

This is a description of the prisoner's helpless condition.

> **He brought them out of darkness and the shadow of death, and brake their bands in sunder.**
>
> **Oh that men would praise the LORD for his goodness, and for his wonderful works to the children of men!**
>
> **For he hath broken the gates of brass, and cut the bars of iron in sunder [Ps. 107:14–16].**

Remember how God brought Simon Peter out of prison and how He delivered Paul and Silas at night. Also He has delivered us from the prison house of sin, and God has given us a pardon. God has a pardon for everyone, my friend. Someone might say, "If there is a pardon, why am I not forgiven?" Well, even in prison today a pardon must be *accepted*. I remember Dr. Harry Rimmer telling about a case in Pennsylvania in which a man was granted a pardon from prison by the governor, but he would not accept it. The prison officials were in a dilemma. What do you do when a man is granted a pardon and he will not accept it? Finally, an appeal was made to the judge, and he said, "The man will have to stay in prison." A person has to *accept* the pardon before he can be free.

The Lord has a pardon for you. In the Lord Jesus Christ we have forgiveness of sins and a pardon for our iniquities, but we have to accept it. Have you accepted your pardon yet? Are you delivered from sin and from the penalty for sin?

This psalm is a marvelous picture of God's mercy, and think what it is going to mean to Israel in the future! Many of them will be in prison, and God will deliver them and bring them back into their land.

THE PROTECTION OF GOD—HE DISSOLVES PROBLEMS

This should be a bass solo. It opens with that same chorus:

> **Oh that men would praise the LORD for his goodness, and for his wonderful works to the children of men! [Ps. 107:21].**

And, my friend, let's do it!

> **And let them sacrifice the sacrifices of thanksgiving, and declare his works with rejoicing [Ps. 107:22].**

God wants you and me to bring an offering of praise and thanksgiving when we come to Him. As a result, "We have an altar, whereof they have no right to eat which serve the tabernacle. For the bodies of those beasts, whose blood is brought into the sanctuary by the high priest for sin, are burned without the camp. Wherefore Jesus also, that he might sanctify the people with his own blood, suffered without the gate. Let us go forth therefore unto him without the camp, bearing his reproach. For here have we no continuing city, but we seek one to come. By him therefore let us offer the sacrifice of praise to God continually, that is, the fruit of our lips giving thanks to his name" (Heb. 13:10–15).

You do not have to wait to go to church to give God a sacrifice: that is, the fruit of your lips giving praise to God. What can you thank Him for? You can thank Him for His protection. He has brought you to this present hour.

> **They that go down to the sea in ships, that do business in great waters;**
>
> **These see the works of the Lord, and his wonders in the deep [Ps. 107:23–24].**

This matter of being a sailor in the days of the psalmist was a dangerous business. A man who went on a voyage couldn't be sure if he was coming back or not. He was more apt to commit himself to God than folk who board a great ship or a plane in our day. Many folk give it no thought at all, or they adopt the philosophy of fatalism and believe their day to die is predetermined. However, it is wonderful to be able to commit ourselves to God at a time like that.

THE POWER OF GOD—HE DELIGHTS HIS PEOPLE

Here now is the final stanza.

> **Oh that men would praise the Lord for his goodness, and for his wonderful works to the children of men! [Ps. 107:31].**

This is a chorus, and we can all join in it because we need God's power in our lives today. It is said of Thomas Aquinas that one day he walked in on the pope while he was counting the money of the church. The pope said, "Sir Thomas, no longer can the church say to the lame man, 'Silver and gold have I none.'" Thomas wheeled around, started out of the room, and without looking back he replied, "That is right, sir. And no longer can the church say to the lame man, 'Rise up and walk.'" Today we are problem conscious, not power conscious. The early church was conscious of the power of God.

Many years ago the Standard Oil Company had a float in the Pasadena Rose Parade. It was a beautiful float—and I shall never forget it—decorated with American Beauty roses, the likes of which I had never seen before. Right in the middle of the parade the float ran out of gas and had to be towed. Everyone laughed, because the Standard Oil Company float is the last one that should have run out of gas! It certainly should have had gas, and enough of it for the parade, but someone had forgotten to fill the tank, and there it was. As I looked at that poor, helpless float, and heard everyone laughing, I felt sorry, because it was like the church of today. We are beautiful, decorated in style with all of our buildings, our programs, our services, and our propaganda, but we have no power. Power is what the church needs, and power is what each individual believer needs. One reason we are powerless is that we are not praising the Lord as we should.

> Let them exalt him also in the congregation of the people, and praise him in the assembly of the elders [Ps. 107:32].

We need to praise God—praise goes before power. It puts gas in the tank and sends the rocket up yonder.

> Whoso is wise, and will observe these things, even they shall understand the lovingkindness of the LORD [Ps. 107:43].

A little girl has defined lovingkindness. She said, "If you ask your mother for a piece of bread and butter, and she gives it to you, that is kindness. But if she puts jam on it without you asking her, that is lovingkindness." My friend, the lovingkindness of God is lavished upon us who belong to Him.

PSALM 108

THEME: Israel's praise and possession

This is another psalm of David, and it is a very wonderful psalm. The first half is the same as Psalm 57, and the last is like Psalm 60. For this reason it has come under criticism and has been judged as a sort of patchwork. However, it is not that at all. If the portions of other psalms have been joined together, God has a purpose in it.

> **O God, my heart is fixed; I will sing and give praise, even with my glory [Ps. 108:1].**

This is Israel's remnant, redeemed, brought home, praising and exalting the Lord. We saw this in the previous psalm. God is going to bring Israel back into the land. He will gather them from all over the world; and, when they are back in the land, they will praise and glorify God.

> **God hath spoken in his holiness; I will rejoice, I will divide Shechem, and mete out the valley of Succoth [Ps. 108:7].**

These, I believe, are the words of the delivered remnant of Israel. They see themselves receiving their inheritance and dividing the land among the tribes. What a time of rejoicing that will be!

PSALM 109

THEME: Messianic—the humiliation of Christ

This psalm, "To the chief Musician, A Psalm of David," is a messianic psalm. It pictures the humiliation of Christ and is an imprecatory psalm. It has been called a Judas Iscariot psalm, because Simon Peter quoted from this psalm in reference to Judas: "For it is written in the book of Psalms, Let his habitation be desolate, and let no man dwell therein: and his bishopric let another take" (Acts 1:20). A "bishopric" is an overseership, and Simon Peter held an election to choose a man to take the place of Judas.

Now notice how this psalm describes Judas Iscariot.

> **Set thou a wicked man over him: and let Satan stand at his right hand.**
>
> **When he shall be judged, let him be condemned: and let his prayer become sin.**
>
> **Let his days be few; and let another take his office.**
>
> **Let his children be fatherless, and his wife a widow [Ps. 109:6–9].**

This indicates that Judas was married and had children.

> **Let his children be continually vagabonds, and beg: let them seek their bread also out of their desolate places [Ps. 109:10].**

You cannot find anything more dreadful than this imprecatory prayer, which was applied to Judas. As far as I know, no one is defending Judas Iscariot. (I have a notion, however, that certain contemporary judges and organizations would have declared Judas innocent and Jesus guilty!) The Word of God is very clear on the subject—Judas was a guilty man, and he was a lost man. This psalm makes the condition of being *lost* frightening. It is a terrible thing to be lost! In fact, the Lord Jesus said, ". . . but woe unto that man by whom the Son of man is betrayed! it had been good for that man if he had not been born" (Matt. 26:24). The Lord Jesus made it very clear that the condition of the lost is a terrible thing. In John 3:36, where He gave that wonderful invitation, He also gave the other side of it; He contrasted light and darkness: "He that believeth on the Son hath everlasting life: and he that believeth not the Son shall not see life; but the wrath of God abideth on him." I don't know how you can make that verse any stronger. The teaching that somehow or other folks who are lost are going to have a second chance, and that there is a larger hope, and that God may have another way, is completely foreign to the Word of God, which says that the wrath of God *abides* on the person who has not trusted Christ. Jesus Christ endured God's wrath for us on the cross. He did it for us, and our only way of salvation is to trust Him. If we do not, God's wrath will be upon us.

PSALM 110

THEME: Messianic—the exaltation of Christ

This psalm, like Psalm 109, is a messianic psalm. It speaks of the exaltation of Christ and begins with the ascension of Christ.

The LORD said unto my Lord, Sit thou at my right hand, until I make thine enemies thy footstool [Ps. 110:1].

This psalm is remarkable because it sets forth the deity of Christ. You could not in any way consider this psalm and still deny His deity. This psalm is referred to many times in the New Testament (Acts 2:34, 35; Heb. 1:13; Heb. 5:6; 6:20; 7:21; 10:12–13).

At the time the enemies of Jesus were making their final onslaught upon Him, the Herodians, a political party, tried to trap Him by forcing Him to make a political statement that would mark Him as a traitor to Rome. When they failed to do that, the Sadducees, a liberal religious party, tried to trap Him with a ridiculous question regarding the Mosaic Law. When they failed, the Pharisees, a religio-political party, tried to trap Him. Jesus' answer puzzled the Pharisees; so while they huddled again to plan further strategy, Jesus asked them a question: "While the Pharisees were gathered together, Jesus asked them, Saying, What think ye of Christ? whose son is he? They say unto him, The son of David. He saith unto them, How then doth David in spirit call him Lord, saying, The LORD said unto my Lord, Sit thou on my right hand, till I make thine enemies thy footstool? If David then call him Lord, how is he his son? And no man was able to answer him a word, neither durst any man from that day forth ask him any more questions" (Matt. 22:41–46). Notice that Jesus asked a straightforward question: "What think ye of Christ?" The Pharisees answered that He was the Son of David. Upon hearing this answer, the Lord pointed them to Psalm 110 to show them their insufficient knowledge of that particular portion of Scripture which the Jews interpreted as messianic. This psalm, written by David, shows Jehovah talking to Messiah. David calls Messiah "my Lord"; and any Jew who admitted Messiah was David's descendant was faced with this psalm, where David calls Messiah his "Lord" and claims that He is superior. This showed that Messiah would be more than a king who would merely be a political ruler upon a throne. Also since David called Him "Lord" in this psalm, how can He be his son? The Lord cannot be his son by natural birth; it had to be by supernatural birth. This psalm is telling us that the Lord Jesus Christ, Israel's Messiah, was virgin born.

"The LORD said unto my Lord. . . ." This is an equal speaking to an equal. This is God speaking to God, if you please. Hebrews 1:13 says, "But to which of the angels said he at any time, Sit on my right hand, until I make thine enemies thy footstool?" This sets forth the deity of Jesus Christ, and it could not be given to us in any stronger fashion. When folk say that the Bible does not teach the deity of Jesus, they are not acquainted with this section of the Word of God, I can assure you.

The LORD shall send the rod of thy strength out of Zion: rule thou in the midst of thine enemies [Ps. 110:2].

This verse speaks of the coming of Christ to the earth to rule in Zion. Concerning this time Isaiah said, "And many people shall go and say, Come ye, and let us go up to the mountain of the LORD, to the house of the God of Jacob; and he will teach us of his ways, and we will walk in his paths: for out of Zion shall go forth the law, and the word of the LORD from Jerusalem" (Isa. 2:3). Jerusalem will be the center of the government on earth. God does have a purpose for Israel in the future.

Thy people shall be willing in the day of thy power, in the beauties of holiness from the womb of the morning: thou hast the dew of thy youth [Ps. 110:3].

During "the day of thy power" there will be the greatest turning to Jesus Christ that the world has ever seen. Spurgeon used to say, "God will have more people saved than there will be lost." It may not look like it today; so don't press your nose up against the window and be discouraged. God may not be doing so well today, but He is not through yet. He has a host of saved folk behind Him, and He has a great many ahead of Him. He has great plans for the future.

The LORD hath sworn, and will not repent, Thou art a priest for ever after the order of Melchizedek [Ps. 110:4].

Here is another very important truth: the Lord Jesus is a High Priest after the order of Melchizedek. This is developed in the Epistle to the Hebrews, because it is one of the greatest truths in the Word of God. At this point let me lift out just one portion from Hebrews: "As he saith also in another place, Thou art a priest for ever after the order of Melchisedec. Who in the days of his flesh, when he had offered up prayers and supplications with strong crying and tears unto him that was able to save him from death, and was heard in that he feared; Though he were a Son, yet learned he obedience by the things which he suffered; And being made perfect, he became the author of eternal salvation unto all them that obey him; Called of God an high priest after the order of Melchisedec" (Heb. 5:6–10). The priesthood of the Lord Jesus is superior to the Aaronic or Levitical priesthood of the Old Testament. These verses show both the deity and the humanity of the Lord Jesus Christ.

The Lord at thy right hand shall strike through kings in the day of his wrath.

He shall judge among the heathen [nations], he shall fill the places with the dead bodies; he shall wound the heads over many countries [Ps. 110:5–6].

You see, Christ is coming again in judgment. As Psalm 2:9 makes clear, "Thou shalt break them with a rod of iron; thou shalt dash them in pieces like a potter's vessel."

He shall drink of the brook in the way: therefore shall he lift up the head [Ps. 110:7].

I like what Dr. Gaebelein says about this verse; so let me quote him: "The passage places before us once more the humiliation and exaltation of our Lord. The humiliation is that He drank of the brook in the way. We are reminded of the three hundred warriors of Gideon, who went down on their knees and lapped water like dogs and who were later used and exalted through victory. But He went deeper than that. He drank of the deep waters of suffering and death. And therefore God has highly exalted Him. What a wonderful Psalm it is!" (*The Book of Psalms*, p. 415).

PSALM 111

THEME: Hallelujah for the works of God

This is a hallelujah psalm for the works of God. And in the Hebrew it is a perfect acrostic, which we don't see in our English translation. This begins a series of three hallelujah psalms (111—113). This psalm praises God for His works and also for His redemption, which is the "new song" that will be sung in heaven. The old song is the song of creation; the new song is the song of redemption. Both are in this psalm.

> **Praise ye the LORD. I will praise the LORD with my whole heart, in the assembly of the upright, and in the congregation [Ps. 111:1].**

"Praise ye the LORD" means Hallelujah. Now notice the works for which He is being praised:

> **The works of the LORD are great, sought out of all them that have pleasure therein.**
>
> **His work is honourable and glorious: and his righteousness endureth for ever.**
>
> **He hath made his wonderful works to be remembered: the LORD is gracious and full of compassion [Ps. 111:2–4].**

The idea today of attributing the origin of this universe to natural causes takes away the glory from God the Father and the Lord Jesus Christ. It is robbing Him of His glory. It is as bad as denying the Lord's redemption or denying Him as Savior. If you accept Him as Savior, you also accept Him as Creator.

Now the psalmist mentions the redemption that we have, which is part of the hallelujah chorus:

> **He sent redemption unto his people: he hath commanded his covenant for ever: holy and reverend is his name [Ps. 111:9].**

Here we find the word *reverend*. The holy God is the reverend God. That title should never be applied to a man. No preacher should be called "Reverend." This is a title for God alone.

God has a redemption for His people.

> **The fear of the LORD is the beginning of wisdom: a good understanding have all they that do his commandments: his praise endureth for ever [Ps. 111:10].**

Oh, my friend, let's praise the Lord for His works. "The works of the LORD are great!" They are great in His creation and display His omnipotence and His eternal wisdom. They are even greater in His redemption, which reveals His righteousness, honor, and glory. Finally the day will come when redemption will be consummated and all things will be put under His feet; then the redeemed nations and creation itself will sing His praise. Hallelujah!

PSALM 112

THEME: *Hallelujah for the righteousness of God*

This is another of the wonderful hallelujah psalms, and it also is written as an acrostic in the Hebrew—which, of course, we miss in our English translations. All twenty-two letters of the Hebrew alphabet are included in this psalm.

The emphasis is on praising God for His righteousness. Because of His righteousness, God must judge sin. Aren't you glad that God is who He is? Suppose He were the Devil and attempted to deceive us and destroy us? It is a horrible thing to even contemplate. But God is *good*. God is *righteous*, and for that very reason He has to deal with sin. The day will come when He will make things right, and I want Him to make things right. I would like the things in my own life to be straightened out, wouldn't you? This is something to praise Him for.

> **Praise ye the LORD. Blessed is the man that feareth the LORD, that delighteth greatly in his commandments [Ps. 112:1].**

Don't despise His commandments. They are a mirror and will let you see who you really are. After broadcasting a series on the Ten Commandments, I received several letters from people who listened to the broadcasts. One man said, "I saw what an awful sinner I was. It was the thing that was separating me from God." A lady wrote and said that her sin was swearing. She would take God's name in vain. Then she turned to the Lord and had a remarkable conversion. It is all because she saw herself in God's mirror. That is what His commandments will do. Don't despise the commandments; but if you are honest, you know that you cannot be saved by keeping them. They reveal that you need a Savior.

Wealth and riches shall be in his house: and his righteousness endureth for ever [Ps. 112:3].

God will never run out of righteousness. He has a good supply of it. Our God is righteous.

Unto the upright there ariseth light in the darkness: he is gracious, and full of compassion, and righteous [Ps. 112:4].

"There ariseth light in the darkness." Why? Because God is gracious, compassionate, and righteous. We really do not know how *good* God is. If we did, we would sing the Hallelujah chorus more often.

Surely he shall not be moved for ever: the righteous shall be in everlasting remembrance [Ps. 112:6].

God is not going to lose sight of His own throughout eternity.

He hath dispersed, he hath given to the poor; his righteousness endureth for ever; his horn shall be exalted with honour [Ps. 112:9].

God is interested in the poor, and He has the only poverty program that is going to work. Unfortunately the Democrats, the Republicans, the Communists, and other groups are not interested in His program. They are going to solve the problem themselves. The real problem is that they do well by *themselves*, instead of doing well by the poor.

The wicked shall see it, and be grieved; he shall gnash with his teeth, and melt away: the desire of the wicked shall perish [Ps. 112:10].

The day is coming when wickedness will end—it will be gone forever. Hallelujah!

PSALM 113

THEME: *A hallelujah chorus to God as Creator and Redeemer*

This psalm to the majesty of God opens the Hallel psalms (113—118), which were sung at the Passover feast, the Feast of Pentecost, the Feast of Tabernacles, and probably at all feasts of Israel. This is a precious and delightful psalm of praise and worship.

> **Praise ye the Lord. Praise, O ye servants of the Lord, praise the name of the Lord [Ps. 113:1].**

We should not take the Lord's name in vain; we should praise the Lord. It is a praise that will never be exhausted because it is to creation's Lord, to creation's Redeemer.

> **Blessed be the name of the Lord from this time forth and for evermore.**
>
> **From the rising of the sun unto the going down of the same Lord's name is to be praised.**
>
> **The Lord is high above all nations, and his glory above the heavens.**
>
> **Who is like unto the Lord our God, who dwelleth on high,**
>
> **Who humbleth himself to behold the things that are in heaven, and in the earth! [Ps. 113:2–6].**

God is so high and lifted up that He has to stoop down in order to look into the heavens!

Now notice what God is going to do:

> **He raiseth up the poor out of the dust, and lifteth the needy out of the dunghill [Ps. 113:7].**

He is the Savior, the Redeemer!

> **That he may set him with princes, even with the princes of his people.**

> **He maketh the barren woman to keep house, and to be a joyful mother of children. Praise ye the Lord [Ps. 113:8-9].**

Hallelujah! Praise the Lord! It is time, my friend, to praise the Lord.

There is one thing I hope to accomplish in this study of the Book of Psalms, and that is to get folk to praise the Lord. Oh, that God's people would *praise* Him! My friend, tell somebody today that God is good, then back it up with your experience of His goodness.

PSALM 114

THEME: God leads His dear children along

This is another of the Hallel psalms (which begin or conclude with a Hallelujah). Psalms 113—118 were called the Egyptian Hallel psalms, and they were used at the Feasts of Passover, Pentecost, Tabernacles and Dedication. Apparently they were sung during the time the Passover was being celebrated. Some Bible scholars think three of them were sung at the beginning and three at the end. Others think they were sung intermittently during the Passover feast.

The psalm before us is a call to praise the wonderful God at whom we have been looking in Psalms 112 and 113. In Psalm 113, for instance, He is the Creator, He is the Redeemer, and He will be the Redeemer of creation. Because of this, we are to praise God. The Hallel psalms are for the purpose of praising God.

Notice that this psalm looks back to the time Israel was delivered from Egyptian bondage.

When Israel went out of Egypt, the house of Jacob from a people of strange language [Ps. 114:1].

When Abraham first went into the Land of Promise, he was a stranger. God told him that his people would go down to the land of Egypt where they would become a nation. Israel began as a nation in Egypt, and anti-Semitism was born in Egypt. The Bible tells of their sufferings, their hardships, their persecutions, and their troubles in Egypt. Then God remembered His covenant with them, heard their cry, looked upon the children of Israel, and had respect unto them. God delivered them from Egypt, and this psalm begins with the wilderness march.

Judah was his sanctuary, and Israel his dominion [Ps. 114:2].

God is speaking now of the whole nation being a tabernacle. God's original intention was that Israel would be a nation of priests—not just one tribe—which means they were to be priests for the world. I think that that is what will happen in the Millennium when Israel will serve in the earthly temple.

> **The sea saw it, and fled: Jordan was driven back [Ps. 114:3].**

The children of Israel not only crossed the Red Sea, they also crossed the Jordan River (Josh. 3:13–17).

> **What ailed thee, O thou sea, that thou fleddest? thou Jordan, that thou wast driven back? [Ps. 114:5].**

The God of creation (whom we saw in Psalm 113 with His omnipotent power) rolled back the Red Sea, and He also held back the waters of Jordan. These were miracles, and I don't think they can be explained on any other basis. When the children of Israel crossed the Red Sea they had been delivered from Egypt by blood—blood on the doorposts. When they crossed over Jordan they were separated from the wilderness and brought into the Promised Land. These are the two stages of redemption, and they illustrate the two stages of our redemption. The Lord Jesus, on the cross, has delivered us from the *penalty* of sin—that is for the past. He delivers us from the *power* of sin in the present—provided we meet His conditions—and He will deliver us from the *presence* of sin, which has not yet been realized. The crossing of the Red Sea and the crossing of the Jordan picture the two stages of redemption.

> **Tremble, thou earth, at the presence of the Lord, at the presence of the God of Jacob;**

**Which turned the rock into a standing water, the flint
into a fountain of waters [Ps. 114:7-8].**

You can see how appropriate the reading of this beautiful little psalm
would be at the celebration of the Passover. It is a call to remembrance
of God's mercy and power on behalf of His people.

PSALM 115

THEME: Glory to God because He is the opposite of heathen idols

This great psalm was sung in the Upper Room at the time our Lord commemorated the Passover with His disciples and instituted the Lord's Supper. It is thrilling to realize that the Lord Jesus Himself sang this and the other Hallel psalms.

We are not told who the writer is, but it is felt that it was written by someone who was celebrating the Remnants return from the Babylonian captivity. It can be divided into three stanzas: (1) the congregation singing (vv. 1–8), (2) the Levites (vv. 9–11), and (3) the congregation (vv. 12–18). You may disagree with me, but it seems to me that it was divided like this.

> **Not unto us, O Lord, not unto us, but unto thy name give glory, for thy mercy, and for thy truth's sake [Ps. 115:1].**

The nation Israel is here taking a very humble place, and they are trusting God. They had not been trusting Him, but they are here in the Great Tribulation and are moving toward the Millennium. You can see that singing this during the three feasts was bound to make an impression upon them.

The heathen round about them were ridiculing them, saying, "Where is your God?"

> **Wherefore should the heathen say, Where is now their God? [Ps. 115:2].**

In other words, "You say He is your God: Why doesn't He deliver you?"

But our God is in the heavens: he hath done whatsoever he hath pleased [Ps. 115:3].

God allowed them to suffer because of their sin. It was according to His will, His plan, and His purpose. Israel is beginning to accept their circumstances from God.

Now listen to his apology against idolatry:

Their idols are silver and gold, the work of men's hands [Ps. 115:4].

Israel's God is in heaven. He is the Creator. He is a spirit. Man did not make Him. The gods of the heathen, on the other hand, were made out of silver and gold; they were the work of men's hands.

They have mouths, but they speak not: eyes have they, but they see not:

They have ears, but they hear not: noses have they, but they smell not [Ps. 115:5–6].

The heathen made their gods with all of the sense organs, but the gods don't use them; indeed, they cannot use them.

They have hands, but they handle not: feet have they, but they walk not: neither speak they through their throat [Ps. 115:7].

In other words, the gods of the heathen cannot help them. Isaiah gave possibly the finest satire against idolatry that you will find in the Scriptures. He says, speaking of men who are idolators, "He heweth him down cedars, and taketh the cypress and the oak, which he strengtheneth for himself among the trees of the forest: he planteth an ash, and the rain doth nourish it. Then shall it be for a man to burn: for he will take thereof, and warm himself; yea, he kindleth it, and baked bread; yea, he maketh a god, and worshippeth it; he maketh it a graven

image, and falleth down thereto. He burneth part thereof in the fire;
with part thereof he eateth flesh; he roasteth roast, and is satisfied:
yea, he warmeth himself, and saith, Aha, I am warm, I have seen the
fire: And the residue thereof he maketh a god, even his graven image:
he falleth down unto it, and worshippeth it, and prayeth unto it, and
saith, Deliver me; for thou art my god" (Isa. 44:14–17). When the idol
is made, the man has to carry it on his back into town. Do you see the
picture? A man is carrying his god. God says to man, "I am the Lord. I
will carry you." Does your God carry you, or do you carry your god? To
many people their religion is a burden, something that they have to
carry on their shoulders. Does God carry you, or do you carry Him? If
you carry Him, that is a modern form of idolatry.

The enemy has ridiculed God's people; now the Levites will answer those who ridicule:

> **O Israel, trust thou in the LORD: he is their help and their
> shield.**
>
> **O house of Aaron, trust in the LORD: he is their help and
> their shield.**
>
> **Ye that fear the LORD, trust in the LORD: he is their help
> and their shield [Ps. 115:9–11].**

Some folks ask me, "What is the answer to atheism? What is the answer to materialism? What is the answer to all of the immorality
around us?" Well, don't bother visiting a psychiatrist and lying on his
couch. He doesn't have the solution. The answer is simple, so simple
that many people have passed right by it: trust the Lord. That's the
solution. In the midst of all the atheism, the materialism, and the immorality, trust the Lord. Rest in Him. Draw near to Him. Cast yourself
upon Him. Oh, this is a wonderful psalm! It will bring you very close
to the Lord.

Beginning with verse 12 the congregation answers. This is, more
or less, an antiphonal psalm.

The LORD hath been mindful of us: he will bless us; he will bless the house of Israel; he will bless the house of Aaron [Ps. 115:12].

God will bless you, too. He will bless your friends, your house, your church, and your community, if only you will turn to Him. The thing that is so wonderful is that He is *mindful* of us. God has not forgotten me, and He has not forgotten you. I don't know your name and address, but He knows it. When I am in an airplane and look down and see all the subdivisions of a city, I think of the thousands of people who live there, and who knows them? Society is very impersonal. You are a number where you work and live; you are a number where you attend school, and you are a number of your government. But God knows you. God not only knows your number, He knows your name, and He knows all about you. Trust in Him.

He will bless them that fear the LORD, both small and great [Ps. 115:13].

This is a categorical, dogmatic statement. Either you believe what it says, or you don't believe it. If you believe it, what a difference it will make in your life!

The LORD shall increase you more and more, you and your children.

Ye are blessed of the LORD which made heaven and earth [Ps. 115:14–15].

He is the Creator.

The heaven, even the heavens, are the LORD'S: but the earth hath he given to the children of men [Ps. 115:16].

Apparently God did not intend for man to live on the moon. When man journeys to the moon, he is more or less using God's property. He has given the earth to man.

**The dead praise not the LORD, neither any that go down
into silence [Ps. 115:17].**

While we are here on earth we are to praise the Lord—here is where it
counts.

**But we will bless the LORD from this time forth and for
evermore. Praise the LORD [Ps. 115:18].**

Those who know Him will bless Him from this time forth and for evermore. Praise the Lord. Hallelujah! You don't mind saying that, do you?
Even if you are a dignified Presbyterian or an Episcopalian, you
should not mind praising the Lord. It won't hurt any of us to do that.
Many of us have tensions and hang-ups. One of the best remedies is to
open your heart to the Lord and praise His name. Talk to Him. It will
help a great deal.

PSALM 116

THEME: *A love song because God swallows death in victory*

This is one of the great psalms in Scripture. Some expositors place it next to Psalm 23 in greatness. It is a psalm of thanksgiving. Man is in distress and calls upon God, and God hears in mercy. It is a love song. It is a Hallel psalm. It is a simple psalm that speaks of the past sufferings of Christ in the presence of death. The night He was arrested and the day before He died the Lord sang this psalm. I wish I could have heard Him sing it! Some folk say they wish they could have heard our Lord speak; I would love to have heard Him sing! It was ". . . for the joy that was set before him [that He] endured the cross . . ." (Heb. 12:2) and He sang that last night with great joy!

It is a psalm that speaks of the future, of the deliverance of the faithful remnant during the Great Tribulation period. Also it speaks of the present and has a message for modern man, for the believer in this hour in which we live. This is what God wants us to know. It is a gracious word for those in distress and trouble. It will relieve your anxiety and dispel your doubts. The Lord Jesus sang this psalm the night before He was crucified. In verses 1–5, God hears. In verses 6–13, God helps. In verses 14–19, God is holy.

GOD HEARS

I love the LORD, because he hath heard my voice and my supplications [Ps. 116:1].

"I love the LORD"—remember that this is a love song. Have you ever told Him that you love Him? I feel that the most important thing in the Christian life is right at this point. Do you love the Lord Jesus? Do you love His person? Do you have a personal relationship with Him? Is there any communication with Him? Have you talked to Him today? Is

He vital and real to you? The world is tired of that which is phony, and aren't you tired of it too? The Scripture says, "We love him, because he first loved us" (1 John 4:19). "Whom having not seen, ye love; in whom, though now ye see him not, yet believing, ye rejoice with joy unspeakable and full of glory" (1 Pet. 1:8). The Lord said to Simon Peter, ". . . Lovest thou me?" (John 21:15–17). ". . . Unto him that loved us, washed us from our sins in his own blood" (Rev. 1:5). To the church in Philadelphia the Lord said, "I will make them to come and worship before thy feet, and to know that I have loved thee" (Rev. 3:9). Philadelphia represents the Bible-believing church today.

Now what is the basis for all of this? "I love the LORD, because he hath heard my voice." Are we to pray audibly? Well, it says, "he hath heard my voice," and that implies audible prayer. I like to talk to the Lord as I drive along in my car. (And, believe me, we need to talk to the Lord as we drive in Southern California these days!)

> **The sorrows of death compassed me, and the pains of hell [sheol] gat hold upon me: I found trouble and sorrow [Ps. 116:3].**

This is the desperate situation of our Lord on the cross. He knew what He would go through—He sang about it the night before He died. Actually the sentence of death was upon us, but it became His sentence. He did not have to die. He laid down His life for you and me. No one took His life from Him.

> **Then called I upon the name of the LORD; O LORD, I beseech thee, deliver my soul [Ps. 116:4].**

He cried out to the Lord, "Save Me." His prayer was heard.

> **Gracious is the LORD, and righteous; yea, our God is merciful [Ps. 116:5].**

God is merciful, but God is righteous. He cannot just arbitrarily forgive sin. He has to be right when He does it. God is the moral Ruler of this universe. He has to be right; He has to be holy; He has to be just, but He also wants to be merciful. The only way was to pay the penalty for the sin of man. Now He says, "Come on, I can receive you."

GOD HELPS

The LORD preserveth the simple: I was brought low, and he helped me.

Return unto thy rest, O my soul; for the LORD hath dealt bountifully with thee [Ps. 116:6–7].

After a difficult, frustrating, pressure-filled day, we need to seek out a quiet place where we can confess our sins, read the Word, and talk with God. That is the sanctuary of the soul. Oh, how all of us need this—"Return unto thy rest, O my soul." This will enable us to walk out and face the world for God.

I will take the cup of salvation, and call upon the name of the LORD [Ps. 116:13].

Apparently this was the Passover cup being passed at this time. As they passed it around the group they would sing, "I will take the cup of salvation." They knew the Passover cup was pointing to the One who was coming. Our Lord sang this in the Upper Room. I have wondered if this was the cup about which He said, "You take this cup and drink it. I'll not take it until I drink it new in the kingdom, because I have a cup to drink tomorrow." Then out in Gethsemane He prayed that the cup would pass from Him. His holy nature rebelled against being made sin. Yet ". . . for the joy that was set before him [he] endured the cross . . ." (Heb. 12:2), and He took that cup joyfully the next day on the cross.

GOD IS HOLY

This brings us to the last section of this psalm which tells us that God is holy. His holiness is important. It is the reason He had to die for us.

**Precious in the sight of the LORD is the death of his saints
[Ps. 116:15].**

Precious was the death of Christ to God. Precious will be the deaths of
those who lay down their lives as martyrs during the Great Tribulation
period, and many will do so. We can apply this today. The death of
God's children is precious in His sight.

**O LORD, truly I am thy servant; I am thy servant, and the
son of thine handmaid: thou hast loosed my bonds.**

**I will offer to thee the sacrifice of thanksgiving, and will
call upon the name of the LORD [Ps. 116:16–17].**

The only thing that you can give God is your thanksgiving. That is *all*
He wants from you. God wants His children to be thankful. Have you
ever thanked Him for your salvation? Have you thanked Him for this
day? Oh, to come to the light of a new day—what a privilege it is!

Forgive me for a personal illustration. When my daughter married
and left home, it was a very difficult time for me. When I watched her
drive off with a "strange" man, I went back over her short life. In my
ministry I have been away from home a great deal. After World War II
when Youth for Christ was really moving, I honestly believed that revival was going to come to our nation. For two years I was never at
home on Saturday night. I spoke for Youth for Christ from border to
border and from coast to coast. I averaged five nights away from home
each week. I recalled one time at the railroad station, as my daughter, a
little tyke then, said to me, "Daddy, either we come down here to tell
you good-bye or to come and get you." Then she looked up at me and
asked, "Can't you stay home more?" Thinking of that, I wrote a letter
to her in which I said, "I feel like I have failed you." A short time later
when my wife and I were in the Hawaiian Islands, I received a letter from her. She wrote, "You did not fail me. I *thank* you for all you did
for me." My friend, I would rather have that thank-you than a check for
a million dollars. There is nothing that she could give me that I want—
just that: "I thank you." Oh, how valuable that is!

My friend, you have nothing that God wants—nothing tangible. The psalmist sings, "I will offer to thee the sacrifice of thanksgiving." I'm going to thank Him. In case we miss the import of this, the writer to the Hebrews says, "By him therefore let us offer the sacrifice of praise to God continually, that is, the fruit of our lips giving thanks to his name" (Heb. 13:15). Oh, my friend, the only thing we can give to our God is our thanks, and how precious that is to our Heavenly Father!

PSALM 117

THEME: Hellelujah for the universal praise of God

This is another Hallel psalm and is the shortest in the series. Let me remind you that the Hallel psalms (113—118) were sung at the three great feasts of the nation Israel: Passover, Pentecost, and Tabernacles.

At the Feast of Passover the cup was passed seven times, and between each passing those gathered would sing one of these hymns. Some expositors say that Psalms 113 and 114 were sung before the meal, and then Psalms 117 and 118 were sung after the meal. It doesn't matter how you arrange them, the important thing is that they were sung. Psalm 118 was the last psalm they sang. Matthew 26:30 tells us, "And when they had sung an hymn, they went out into the mount of Olives."

This is not only the shortest psalm, it is the shortest chapter in the Bible. Because of that there is a danger of passing over it altogether.

> **O praise the Lord, all ye nations: praise him, all ye people [Ps. 117:1].**

"Praise the Lord" is "hallelujah."

> **For his merciful kindness is great toward us: and the truth of the Lord endureth for ever. Praise ye the Lord [Ps. 117:2].**

These are remarkable verses that we should not pass over hurriedly. "Praise the Lord, all ye nations" is obviously prophetic. It looks to the future when all nations and races and tribes and tongues on every continent and in every nation will join together in praising Jehovah and will worship Him as Lord. Is there anything like that in the world today? Do you see any evidence of it in your neighborhood? Can you see that the world is turning to God? There was a time at the turn of the century, during the good old Victorian era and during the Gay Nineties, when it was thought that the Millennium was about to be ushered in. That was the heyday of postmillennialism, and a premillennialist in that day had to run for cover. They would have ridden anyone out of town on a rail who would have been pessimistic enough to say that a time of Great Tribulation was going to come upon the world! "Praise the LORD, all ye nations." I have a question to ask: Where are the nations that are singing praises unto Jehovah today? Where are the nations who worship and adore Him and are in submission to Him? The answer is easy—there are no nations today that fit that description. The message of the prophets was that one day the nations would praise and worship the Lord. In Zechariah 2:11 it says, "And many nations shall be joined to the LORD in that day, and shall be my people. . . ." Then in Zechariah 14:16 we read, "And it shall come to pass, that every one that is left of all the nations which came against Jerusalem shall even go up from year to year to worship the King, the LORD of hosts, and to keep the feast of tabernacles." Evidently the worshipping of all nations is connected with the turning of Israel to God.

The next question is, When will all of this find fulfillment? I think the answer to that is in this little psalm before us. When will the nations praise Jehovah? Notice what it says in verse 2: "For his merciful kindness is great toward us." Who is the "us" in this phrase? It is Israel. The day is coming when God is going to be gracious to Israel. That day is in the future, at the end of the Great Tribulation period, when the Lord comes to earth for the second time and establishes His kingdom. Then He will be gracious to Israel and to all the nations on the earth. At that time Micah says (referring to God), "Thou wilt perform the truth to Jacob, and the mercy to Abraham, which thou hast sworn unto our fathers from the days of old" (Mic. 7:20). Then in Isaiah 54:7–8 we read, "For a small moment have I forsaken thee; but with great mercies will I gather thee. In a little wrath I hid my face from thee for a moment; but with everlasting kindness will I have mercy on thee, saith the LORD thy Redeemer." So, my friend, you can see that this psalm has reference to a future day when all the nations are going to praise the Lord.

Is there any inkling of this subject in the New Testament? Yes, Acts 15 records the meeting of the council at Jerusalem, which was made up of Jewish believers; and they could not understand why the prophecies of the Old Testament were not being fulfilled. At the end of the conference James got up and said, "Simeon hath declared how God at the first did visit the Gentiles, to take out of them a people for his name" (Acts 15:14). My friend, that is what God is doing in our day—taking out a people from among the Gentiles. He is making up His church from all races and tribes and tongues and bringing them together into one body. Now notice how James continues, "And to this agree the words of the prophets; as it is written. After this"—after what? After He takes the church out of the world. "I will return, and will build again the tabernacle of David, which is fallen down; and I will build again the ruins thereof, and I will set it up: That the residue of men might seek after the Lord, and all the Gentiles, upon whom my name is called, saith the Lord, who doeth all these things" (Acts 15:15–17). As you can see, the psalm before us looks to the future when every creature on this earth will render praise unto God.

It simply is not true that the nations today are praising God. You may see some evidence of it in your little corner of the world; but, in my little corner in Southern California, there is no evidence that everyone will turn to God. However, the time is coming when "God shall bless us; and all the ends of the earth shall fear him" (Ps. 67:7).

Psalm 117 is a tremendous psalm. It is like an atom bomb in the midst of the psalms, and when this little bomb explodes, you won't find a postmillennialist or an amillennialist anywhere, for it will blow them all away. The fulfillment of this psalm will come during the Millennium when Christ reigns on this earth—and not before. Oh, what a glorious time that will be! "Praise ye the Lord"—Hallelujah!

PSALM 118

THEME: The hymn Christ sang with His disciples before His death

This wonderful psalm is the last of the Hallel psalms; for this reason we know it was the psalm which our Lord sang with His disciples the night before His death.

In the Upper Room that night there was an air of informality but also of awe, an air of sadness and of joy and of anticipation. Our Lord ate the Passover feast with His disciples; then on the dying embers of a fading feast, He reared something new. Out of the ashes of the past, He took frail elements—bread and grape juice which will spoil in a few days, the weakest things in the world—and He raised a monument. It is not of marble, not of bronze, silver, or gold; it is bread and juice. That's all. But it speaks of Him. We know from the Old Testament that a lamb was to be eaten at the Passover feast. But in the Gospel record we hear nothing about the lamb, only the bread and fruit of the vine. Do you know why? It is because the Lamb was there serving them. He was on the way to the cross as the Lamb of God to die, and the bread and juice were to speak of Him until He comes again.

Psalm 118 is the psalm they sang together on that fatal night. The Gospels tell us, "When they had sung an hymn, they went out . . ." (Matt. 26:30). It is Psalm 118, which makes this psalm very important to us.

It is said that at the Passover feast, the cup went around the circle seven times. The seventh time it came to Him, our Lord said, "I'll not drink this cup with you," and He passed it on. "I'll drink it new with you in my Father's kingdom." He had already said that He would take the cup of salvation—and He took it yonder on the cross. Christ is the Lamb of God who shed His blood, and the cup is the new covenant of His blood. He drank the bitter cup that our cup might be sweet. Oh, how good God is to us!

> O give thanks unto the LORD; for he is good: because his mercy endureth for ever.
>
> Let Israel now say, that his mercy endureth for ever.
>
> Let the house of Aaron now say, that his mercy endureth for ever [Ps. 118:1–3].

And let Vernon McGee now say that His mercy endureth for ever. And let you say that His mercy endureth for ever. Let us all "give thanks unto the LORD, for he is good."

> Let them now that fear the LORD say, that his mercy endureth for ever.
>
> I called upon the LORD in distress: the LORD answered me, and set me in a large place.
>
> The LORD is on my side; I will not fear: what can man do unto me? [Ps. 118:4–6].

This is the song that our Lord sang. He went to the cross without fear. And He cried out, ". . . My God, my God, why hast thou forsaken me?" (Matt. 27:46). The mystery of it all is ". . . that God was in Christ, reconciling the world unto himself . . ." (2 Cor. 5:19).

> The LORD taketh my part with them that help me: therefore shall I see my desire upon them that hate me.
>
> It is better to trust in the LORD than to put confidence in man [Ps. 118:7–8].

Have you learned to put your confidence in the Lord, rather than in man? It is a marvelous lesson to learn. A prominent Los Angeles attorney and outstanding jurist told me, "When I was a young Christian, my Christian life was almost ruined. I had my eye on a man, and that man failed me. I found out then that I had made a mistake. I cannot put confidence in men." The psalmist says that it is better to trust in the

Lord than to put confidence in man. On the night that our Lord sang
these words He looked around at eleven men. One of them had already
gone to betray Him. Those eleven men were going to forsake Him—
they would be scattered like sheep that night. Don't put your confidence in men, my friend, they will let you down. Put your trust in the
Lord.

> It is better to trust in the Lord than to put confidence in
> princes.
>
> All nations compassed me about: but in the name of the
> Lord will I destroy them.
>
> They compassed me about; yea, they compassed me
> about: but in the name of the Lord I will destroy them.
>
> They compassed me about like bees; they are quenched
> as the fire of thorns: for in the name of the Lord I will
> destroy them [Ps. 118:9–12].

"All nations compassed me about"—Rome was a polyglot nation, and
Rome nailed our Lord to a cross. The day He died on a Roman cross,
that nation was doomed. Its days were numbered. That great world
empire that had existed for a millennium would pass off the stage of
human events. (It will, however, come back by the way of Antichrist.)

> The Lord is my strength and song, and is become my
> salvation [Ps. 118:14].

In this wonderful section we have praise for deliverance. It is a song of
salvation.

> The voice of rejoicing and salvation is in the tabernacles
> of the righteous: the right hand of the Lord doeth val-
> iantly.
>
> The right hand of the Lord is exalted: the right hand of
> the Lord doeth valiantly.

> **I shall not die, but live, and declare the works of the
> LORD [Ps. 118:15–17].**

This is a reference to our Lord's resurrection. Also there is something else here: Israel is going to survive as a nation.

> **The LORD hath chastened me sore: but he hath not given
> me over unto death [Ps. 118:18].**

That is, Christ came back from the dead. And Ezekiel 37 makes it clear that God will open the graves and bring out the nations of the world.

> **Open to me the gates of righteousness: I will go into
> them, and I will praise the LORD:**
>
> **This gate of the LORD, into which the righteous shall en-
> ter [Ps. 118:19–20].**

What is the gate of the Lord? Christ made it very clear when He said, "I am the door: by me if any man enter in, he shall be saved, and shall go in and out, and find pasture" (John 10:9). That door was the door to the sheepfold. The Lord also said, ". . . I am the way, the truth, and the life: no man cometh unto the Father, but by me" (John 14:6).

> **I will praise thee: for thou hast heard me, and art be-
> come my salvation [Ps. 118:21].**

Now we have another figure of speech:

> **The stone which the builders refused is become the head
> stone of the corner [Ps. 118:22].**

The stone in this verse refers to Christ Himself. Our Lord in Matthew 21:42 made that clear: ". . . Did ye never read in the scriptures, The stone which the builders rejected, the same is become the head of the corner: this is the Lord's doing, and it is marvellous in our eyes?" First

Peter 2:6–8 says, "Wherefore also it is contained in the scripture, Behold I lay in Zion a chief corner stone, elect, precious: and he that believeth on him shall not be confounded. Unto you therefore which believe he is precious: but unto them which be disobedient, the stone which the builders disallowed, the same is made the head of the corner, And a stone of stumbling, and a rock of offense, even to them which stumble at the word, being disobedient: whereunto also they were appointed." The stone is the Lord Jesus Christ.

> **This is the day which the Lord hath made; we will rejoice and be glad in it [Ps. 118:24].**

What *day* is the psalmist talking about—some twenty-four-hour day? No. The word *day* can be used for a period of time, it can be used for a twenty-four-hour day, and it can be used for a peculiar type of thing—most anything. For example, we could say that this is the *day* of the automobile. Now what *day* is the psalmist referring to here? Well, he is talking about the day "which the Lord hath made," the day of salvation. That *day* has already been two thousand years long, and "we will rejoice and be glad in it." We rejoice in the day of salvation.

Now here we have the believing cry, Hosanna—"Save now" is the word *hosanna*. It is the word the multitudes used when our Lord came riding into Jerusalem:

> **Save now, I beseech thee, O Lord: O Lord, I beseech thee, send now prosperity.**

> **Blessed be he that cometh in the name of the Lord: we have blessed you out of the house of the Lord [Ps. 118:25–26].**

"Blessed be he that cometh in the name of the Lord" was quoted by our Lord after He cleansed the temple for the final time, then wept over Jerusalem. His words were, "Behold, your house is left unto you desolate. For I say unto you, Ye shall not see me henceforth, till ye shall say, Blessed is he that cometh in the name of the Lord" (Matt. 23:38–39).

> **God is the LORD, which hath shewed us light: bind the sacrifice with cords, even unto the horns of the altar [Ps. 118:27].**

This is a picture of the Lord Jesus Christ on the cross, a sacrifice for you and for me.

> **Thou art my God, and I will praise thee: thou art my God, I will exalt thee.**

> **O give thanks unto the LORD; for he is good: for his mercy endureth for ever [Ps. 118:28–29].**

My friend, I wish I could somehow express to you the fact that you and I ought to praise the Lord. In my flesh I am cabined and contained and have all kinds of hang-ups. I wish I could open up like a flower and express my praise and thanksgiving to my God! Oh, my friend, to fall down and worship Him, to praise *His* name and glorify *Him* is all important. He loved us and gave Himself for us. May our love today go out to him in adoration and praise.

PSALM 119

THEME: Praise to the Word of God

W e come now to the longest psalm and the longest chapter in the
Bible. It has in it 176 verses, and every verse (with the possible
exception of two verses) is praise to the Word of God. Oh, that you and
I might put an emphasis upon the Word of God. As believers, we need
to put the emphasis where God puts it. In our day there is too much
emphasis upon programs and methods and ceremonies and church
activities. Our emphasis should be on the Word of God, because that is
the only thing He has promised to bless. He has never promised to
bless me or my ministry or any other ministry, but He has promised to
bless His Word.

The mechanics of this psalm, the arrangement of it, is indeed interesting. It was written with a great deal of care. It is an acrostic, but an
acrostic that is a little different from any that we have seen before. Instead of having one verse that begins with each letter of the Hebrew
alphabet (there are twenty-two letters in the Hebrew alphabet), there
are eight verses for each letter of the Hebrew alphabet, beginning with
Aleph, Beth, Gimel, and so forth, which gives us 176 verses in this
psalm.

There are Bible students who feel that numbers in the Bible are
very significant. I don't want to labor the point, but I do find it interesting that eight is the key number in this psalm, because under each
letter of the Hebrew alphabet there are eight verses. The number eight
in Scripture seems to be the number of resurrection. It was on the
eighth day that our Lord came back from the dead—He was dead on
the seventh day, the sabbath, and the eighth day, the first day of the
week, He was resurrected. Many people think that God is through
with Israel, but He is not through with them. Paul made that very clear
in Romans 11:15: "For if the casting away of them be the reconciling of
the world, what shall the receiving of them be, but life from the
dead?" God is definitely not through with Israel. Just as the Lord Jesus

came back from the dead, these people will be brought back as a nation in the Millennium. God would, in a very special way, save nations— oh, the multitudes that are yet to be saved! Spurgeon used to say, "God is going to win. There will be more saved than there will be lost." I believe that with all my heart, although as I look around me today I don't see it happening.

Many people get excited when they visit the land of Israel today, thinking they are seeing the fulfillment of prophecy. While it is true that Jews are returning to the land of Israel, it is not a fulfillment of Scripture, because they are returning in unbelief; they are not turning to God. I read recently of Jewish immigrants to Israel who were shocked by the atheism and lack of observance of the Jewish religion in Israel. It is true that there is no more a turning to God in Jerusalem than there is in my hometown or your hometown. But when God fulfills His prophecy, He will bring the Jews back to their land and it will be a resurrection of the nation, life from the dead. And, my friend, if you receive life from the dead—if you receive eternal life—it will come through the Word of God. "Being born again, not of corruptible seed, but of incorruptible, by the word of God, which liveth and abideth for ever" (1 Pet. 1:23). We are begotten by the Word of God that reveals Jesus Christ. God's Word will bring life to you, it will bring liberty to you, it will bring joy to you, and it will bring blessing to you.

This psalm has meant a great deal to believers down through the years. Late in life John Ruskin wrote, "It is strange that of all the pieces of the Bible which my mother taught me, that which cost me the most to learn, and which was to my childish mind most repulsive—the 119th Psalm—has now become of all the most precious to me in its overflowing and glorious passion of love for the Law of God."

William Wilberfore, the statesman who was converted in the Wesleyan movement, wrote in his diary, "Walked from Hyde Park corner, repeating the 119th Psalm in great comfort." What a wonderful statement. If you can't sleep at night, don't count sheep; count the letters of the Hebrew alphabet and read the verses of this psalm. It would mean a great deal to you.

In this wonderful psalm God's Word is designated by several terms:

word, saying, way, testimonies, judgments, precepts, commandments, law, statutes, and faithfulness.

As we go through this psalm, I will lift out certain verses. We will begin with *Aleph* which is the first letter of the Hebrew alphabet.

ALEPH

Blessed are the undefiled in the way, who walk in the law of the LORD,

Blessed are they that keep his testimonies, and that seek him with the whole heart [Ps. 119:1–2].

Oh, that we would seek God with the whole heart—not halfheartedly. I get a little discouraged with some folk who start out with our "Thru the Bible" program with a great deal of zeal at first. Then they begin to let down, and before long they drop by the wayside. They are not like the man in Psalm 1:1, of whom it is said, "Blessed is the man that walketh not in the counsel of the ungodly, nor standeth in the way of sinners, nor sitteth in the seat of the scornful." Blessed is the man that walketh not, standeth not, sitteth not, but just keeps on walking— walking in the Spirit. "Blessed are they that keep his testimonies, and that seek him with the whole heart."

BETH

Wherewithal shall a young man cleanse his way? by taking heed thereto according to thy word [Ps. 119:9].

One thing that every young man should learn about today is the Word of God. They are taught everything else in school except the Bible. It is against the law to teach the Bible in school, but we need to get the Word of God to them.

Thy word have I hid in mine heart, that I might not sin against thee [Ps. 119:11].

Many people believe that this verse only means that Scripture should
be memorized. I think memorizing God's Word is a wonderful thing,
but some of the meanest little brats I have seen in Sunday school were
the ones who could stand up and quote one hundred verses of Scripture. When the psalmist wrote, "Thy word have I hid in mine heart," I
think he meant, "I obey it." That is the important thing. It is a wonderful thing to be able to stand up and by rote recite verse after verse—I'm
not criticizing that; I'm in favor of Scripture memorization programs—
but we also need to *obey* the Word. That is what the psalmist means by
hiding it in your heart.

GIMEL

**Open thou mine eyes, that I may behold wondrous
things out of thy law [Ps. 119:18].**

This is the verse I used to begin the "Thru the Bible" program years
ago when I first taught it in a little weather-beaten church on the side of
a red clay hill in Georgia. I used this verse as a theme for many years.
This is a good one—"Open thou mine eyes, that I may behold wondrous things out of thy law [thy word]."

DALETH

In the *Daleth* section we read:

**My soul cleaveth unto the dust: quicken thou me accord-
ing to thy word [Ps. 119:25].**

The tendency today is to pull downward. Everything pulls us down.
Television—a marvelous instrument that could be used for God—does
nothing but pull us down. Everything is geared that way. "My soul
cleaveth unto the dust"—we gravitate in that direction. Not only will
our body fall downward, but our soul is pulled downward in the
world. How can we overcome it? "Quicken [revive] thou me according
to thy word." This is another reason I have a five-year program of going

through the Bible. If folk will stay in the Word of God for five years, it will keep them out of a lot of sin. The Word will revive us and lift us up.

HE

In the *He* section we read:

> Teach me, O LORD, the way of thy statutes; and I shall keep it unto the end [Ps. 119:33].

Oh, to follow on with God, running the race with patience, looking unto Jesus.

VAU

> Let thy mercies come also unto me, O LORD, even thy salvation, according to thy word [Ps. 119:41].

God's mercy is channeled to us—the pipe that brings it to us is the Word of God. Therefore, the psalmist says:

> And I will delight myself in thy commandments, which I have loved [Ps. 119:47].

Does it give you joy to read the Word of God? Do you love the Bible? If you don't love God's Word, ask Him to give you a love for it. I did that for years. I prayed, "Lord, give me a love for your Word." I was not brought up in a home where I heard the Word of God, and it took me a long time to become interested in it.

ZAIN

> Remember the word unto thy servant, upon which thou hast caused me to hope [Ps. 119:49].

In other words, "Fulfill thy promises to me, upon which thou hast caused me to hope."

CHETH

Thou art my portion, O Lord: I have said that I would keep thy words [Ps. 119:57].

This is literally, "My portion O Lord!" Spurgeon comments: "The poet is lost in wonder while he sees that the great and glorious God is all his own! Well, might he be so, for there is no possession like Jehovah himself."

At midnight I will rise to give thanks unto thee because of thy righteous judgments [Ps. 119:62].

Have you ever thanked God in the middle of the night for His Word? Well, wake up tonight and do it.

TETH

The proud have forged a lie against me: but I will keep thy precepts with my whole heart.

Their heart is as fat as grease; but I delight in thy law [Ps. 119:69–70].

Critics of the Bible need to go on a diet, or they may die of heart trouble. We need to stay close to the Word of God. It is marvelous for heart trouble!

JOD

Thy hands have made me and fashioned me: give me understanding, that I may learn thy commandments [Ps. 119:73].

God made us. He knows exactly what we need. One of our basic needs is His Word, and that is what the psalmist is talking about here. I notice that some of the manufacturers of automobiles say, "When your car needs repair, take it to us. We made it, and we know how to fix it." Well, that may be good advice also. I know for sure that you need to take yourself to the Lord and to His Word. He made you, and He knows what is good for you.

CAPH

This psalm speaks of one persecuted but not forsaken—

> **For I am become like a bottle in the smoke; yet do I not forget thy statutes [Ps. 119:83].**

"A bottle in the smoke" undoubtedly refers to a wine skin "bottle" hung up in the fire, which would become blackened, parched, and cracked. What a picture of the one who endures long and severe persecution! But he was not forsaken because the Word of God was his stay.

LAMED

> **For ever, O LORD, thy word is settled in heaven [Ps. 119:89].**

I have preached on this verse many times. "For ever, O LORD, thy word is settled in heaven"—His Word is in heaven; that is where the original copy is. I believe in the plenary, verbal inspiration of that copy, and I hold a good copy of it right in my hands. Actually it is settled in the *heavens*. Now heaven and earth may pass away, but where He is, it will never pass away.

MEM

> **O how love I thy law! It is my meditation all the day [Ps. 119:97].**

He meditated in God's Word because he loved it, and then he loved it even more because he meditated in it.

> **I have more understanding than all my teachers: for thy testimonies are my meditation [Ps. 119:99].**

When I taught a course in Bible at a Bible institute, I used to tell my students, "Don't you ever give me this verse or I'll give you an F in the course!" Seriously, humble believers who sit at the feet of Christ are often more skilled in the Word than a man who has a D.D. or a Ph.D. after his name.

NUN

Now here is a verse you may have heard all your life—

> **Thy word is a lamp unto my feet, and a light unto my path [Ps. 119:105].**

Each of us should use the Word of God personally, practically, and habitually as we make our way through this dark world.

SAMECH

Now, again, let me lift out only one verse from this section:

> **I hate vain thoughts: but thy law do I love [Ps. 119:113].**

How much time do you spend reading the newspaper, or reading trash, in comparison to the time that you spend reading the Bible? God is telling us, through the psalmist, that He hates vain thoughts. If you spend time in the Word of God, the day will come when you will not be interested in a lot of the trash that is published.

AIN

It is time for thee, LORD, to work: for they have made void thy law [Ps. 119:126].

This is a good prayer for us to pray today. I pray this prayer, "Lord, the world has forgotten you, and the world has forgotten your Word. Help us get it out today, and make the world conscious of your Word."

PE

Thy testimonies are wonderful: therefore doth my soul keep them [Ps. 119:129].

"Thy testimonies are wonderful"—full of wonderful revelations, commands, and promises. As Spurgeon has well said, "Jesus the eternal Word is called Wonderful, and all the uttered words of God are wonderful in their degree. Those who know them best wonder at them most."

The entrance of thy words giveth light; it giveth understanding unto the simple [Ps. 119:130].

Since I come under that classification, I want to know the Word.

TZADDI

Righteous art thou, O LORD, and upright are thy judgments [Ps. 119:137].

"Righteous art thou, O LORD"—we can rest in the truth of that when we cannot see the reasons for our trials and troubles. We may be confident of this sure and certain fact that God is righteous and His dealings with us are also righteous.

KOPH

I cried with my whole heart; hear me, O LORD: I will keep thy statutes.

I cried unto thee; save me, and I shall keep thy testimonies [Ps. 119:145–146].

When God saves you, He wants to put you on a new diet, a diet of the Word of God.

RESH

Plead my cause, and deliver me: quicken me according to thy word [Ps. 119:154].

The word quicken is better translated "revive." So the psalmist is saying, "Revive me according to Thy Word." The only thing that can revive us is God's Word. Dwight L. Moody said that the next great revival will be a revival of the Word of God. I hope that that is true, and we are seeing more and more interest in the Bible.

SCHIN

Princes have persecuted me without a cause: but my heart standeth in awe of thy word [Ps. 119:161].

The psalmist had more respect and awe for the Word of God than he did for the rulers of this word.

TAU

I have gone astray like a lost sheep; seek thy servant; for I do not forget thy commandments [Ps. 119:176].

As long as the Word of God is in your heart, my friend, as long as there is a longing deep within you to come to God, the Shepherd is out looking for you. He will put you on His shoulder and bring you back into the fold.

Psalm 119 is a glorious psalm. It glorifies the Word of God which is the foundation of all liberty. And it reveals the Savior—"If the Son therefore shall make you free, ye shall be free indeed" (John 8:36). Oh, what liberty the Word of God will give to your heart and life!

PSALM 120

THEME: *The living conditions of the pilgrim*

This brings us to a new series in the Book of Psalms, a package of fifteen psalms (120—134), each called "A song of degrees" in our Bibles. What we have here is, as Martin Luther translated it, the gradual psalms, songs of the higher choir. An outstanding Hebrew scholar has translated it, "Songs of the pilgrim caravans" or "on the homeward marches." These fifteen psalms were traveling songs, and I think they were used in two different ways. When the captives returned from Babylon, they sang them on the way to Jerusalem. This same use of the term "going up" is used in Ezra 7:9, which says, "For upon the first day of the first month began he [that is, Ezra] to go up from Babylon, and on the first day of the fifth month came he to Jerusalem, according to the good hand of his God upon him." This verse is speaking of Ezra's "going up" from Babylon to Jerusalem. However the most common use of these psalms was during the three times each year when they went, as God had commanded, up to Jerusalem to worship. God had required the males to go; and, when they went, they took their families along. As they started to Jerusalem from all over the civilized world—they were scattered at this time—they would sing these psalms. One day it would be one of the psalms, the next day another psalm; and as they came closer and higher, as they approached Jerusalem, they continued to sing them until they came to the final psalm, 134, when they would be standing in the sanctuary of the Lord singing His praises. This is the reason they are called songs of degrees or ascents and songs of the pilgrim caravans. You will recall that we have one incident, recorded by Dr. Luke, in the life of the Lord Jesus between the time of His virgin birth and the beginning of His ministry at the age of thirty years. The Lord, who was then twelve years old, went with His parents to Jerusalem to celebrate one of the feasts. A day's journey from Jerusalem, all of the caravans would meet so that they could go to Jerusalem together. It was a time of fellowship, of renewing friendships, talking over old times, and telling others how things were going. Then they would journey together to Jerusalem, singing these psalms. The place where the caravans met is still pretty well known today, and it was one day's journey out of Jerusalem. When the feast was over, the parents of the Lord Jesus found He was missing, and they had to return to the city to look for Him. The account is found in Luke 2:41–50.

Now you may be wondering if we can be sure these psalms were used this way. Yes, Psalm 122:3–4 gives us this information: "Jerusalem is builded as a city that is compact together: Whither the tribes go up, the tribes of the LORD, unto the testimony of Israel, to give thanks unto the name of the LORD." Yes, they were sung three times during the year—at the Feasts of Passover, Pentecost, and Tabernacles—as they traveled toward Jerusalem to return thanks to God, to worship Him, and to offer sacrifices.

There is a spiritual meaning in these fifteen psalms. It is interesting that many writers of the Talmud pointed out the fact that life is like this—it is an ascent. We come to God as sinners who are away from Him, separated, and alienated. We come to Him for salvation, and having come for salvation, we go on to sanctification as we grow in grace and in the knowledge of Christ; it is a constant going up. We are to be climbing in a spiritual way. My friend, you and I ought to be farther along today than we were last year.

Now we begin this journey with Psalm 120, and in this psalm we are looking at the pilgrim and we will find out where he lives.

> **In my distress I cried unto the LORD, and he heard me.**
>
> **Deliver my soul, O LORD, from lying lips, and from a deceitful tongue.**
>
> **What shall be given unto thee? or what shall be done unto thee, thou false tongue?**
>
> **Sharp arrows of the mighty, with coals of juniper.**
>
> **Woe is me, that I sojourn in Mesech, that I dwell in the tents of Kedar!**

My soul hath long dwelt with him that hateth peace.

I am for peace: but when I speak, they are for war [Ps. 120:1–7].

This is one of the most marvelous psalms that we have read, and it is relevant to the present hour, especially for the nation Israel. The pilgrim in this psalm said he lived "in Mesech in Kedar." Who was Mesech? He was one of the sons of Japheth. Genesis 10:2 tells us of "The sons of Japheth; Gomer, and Magog, and Madai, and Javan, and Tubal, and Meshech, and Tiras." From the sons of Japheth came the gentile nations, and Israel today is scattered among the Gentiles throughout the world. They dwell in "Mesech." "Kedar" was the son of Ishmael. Does that tell you anything? The pilgrim was living among the Arabs. That is rather up-to-date, is it not?

Notice that in verse 2 he cries, "Deliver my soul, O LORD, from lying lips, and from a deceitful tongue." It doesn't sound as if he is living in a good neighborhood, does it? They had mean tongues. The man who sojourned in Mesech had been maligned and lied about. I do believe that no people have been lied about, maligned, and persecuted as much as the Jews. We hear much about minority groups today, and the interesting thing is that the Jew has been able to make his way among all nations and peoples, but he has been criticized the entire time. Anti-Semitism has been real down through the ages; yet the Jew has been able to survive all of it. The Jews are a minority group among the Gentiles and among the people of the world; and they have lived in the place of gossip, quarrels, tensions, problems, and burdens. Also this can be said of you and me.

Now, not only did the pilgrim live among people with mean tongues, but he lived in a world of war: "My soul hath long dwelt with him that hateth peace. I am for peace: but when I speak, they are for war." That is rather up-to-date also, is it not? It is a wonder the higher critics, who like to give a late dating to Scripture, haven't suggested that this psalm was written in the present century. It certainly describes the Jews' current situation.

Now it is time to pack up his troubles in his old kit bag and start toward Jerusalem. However, the pilgrim leaves his burdens at home. He leaves his Mesech and his Kedar and starts for Jerusalem to worship his God. Jerusalem is the city of peace. It is not that today; it is rather a dangerous place to be, but it was different in the days of the pilgrim, and it will be different in the future.

PSALM 121

THEME: The pilgrim sees the hills of Judea come into view

This psalm is the next "song of degrees" or song of ascents as the pilgrim travels to Jerusalem to worship. We had a glimpse into his home situation which he had left as he started on his way. Now in this psalm he can see in the distance the hills of Jerusalem.

I will lift up mine eyes unto the hills, from whence cometh my help [Ps. 121:1].

I think it would be well to change this verse because it is obviously a question rather than a statement. This man is not looking to the hills for his help; he is looking to God. "Shall I lift my eyes unto the hills? From whence cometh my help?" His answer is in the next verse:

My help cometh from the LORD which made heaven and earth [Ps. 121:2].

His help comes from God, and not from the hills.

As the pilgrim draws near to Jerusalem, and it makes no difference if he comes from the north, east, south, or west, he will have to go through hills. The first time I went to Jerusalem, I came from the east, across the Jordan River; and I traveled through some pretty rugged country. The second time I went to Jerusalem, I came from Tel Aviv by bus and found that the hills were "hillier" than they were on the east. I have also approached Jerusalem from the north and south—no matter from what direction you approach Jerusalem, you are in the hills.

As the pilgrim comes to the place where he can see the hills of Judea, he sees places of heathen worship on the tops of the hills. That is where the heathen erected their altars. He says, "Shall I lift up mine eyes to the hills? From whence cometh my help?" It doesn't come from the tops of those hills. Jeremiah commented on this subject when he said, "Truly in vain is salvation hoped for from the hills, and from the multitude of mountains: truly in the LORD our God is the salvation of Israel" (Jer. 3:23). This is in the song of the pilgrim as he draws near Jerusalem.

> **He will not suffer thy foot to be moved: he that keepeth thee will not slumber.**
>
> **Behold, he that keepeth Israel shall neither slumber nor sleep [Ps. 121:3–4].**

"He will not suffer thy foot to be moved" means that God won't allow you to totter. Those of us who are senior citizens begin to totter just a little—I notice that I am not as surefooted as I once was.

> **The sun shall not smite thee by day, nor the moon by night.**
>
> **The LORD shall preserve thee from all evil: he shall preserve thy soul.**
>
> **The LORD shall preserve thy going out and thy coming in from this time forth, and even for evermore [Ps. 121:6–8].**

I would like to give you a different translation of verses 3–8 which will bring out something not seen in the King James Version. "He will not suffer thy foot to be moved: thy keeper will not slumber. Behold, neither slumbereth nor sleepeth the keeper of Israel. Jehovah is thy keeper. Jehovah is thy shade upon the right hand: the sun shall not smite thee by day nor the moon by night. The Lord shall keep thee from all evil. He shall keep thy soul. Jehovah shall keep thy going out and thy coming in from henceforth and forever" (Translation mine). This pilgrim is not looking to the hills for strength. He is looking to the Lord for help. Jehovah is his keeper.

You will notice that in verses 7 and 8 we are told that "the LORD shall preserve thee." This has to do with the wonderful keeping power of God. He preserves you. Peter said it like this, "Who are kept by the power of God . . ." (1 Pet. 1:5). There are two ways to preserve fruits or vegetables—in sugar or in vinegar. Many Christians are preserved both ways. Those preserved in sugar are nice sweet folks. The others are preserved in vinegar, and that speaks for itself.

The pilgrim is moving toward Jerusalem. He travels through the hills and camps along the route. Howard Johnson, the Holiday Inn, and the Ramada Inn hadn't built any motels yet; so the travelers going to Jerusalem had to camp along the way. And they were looking to Jehovah to keep them. What a glorious assurance that is! The psalm says, "My help cometh from the LORD. He won't let me totter and fall." There are other references to this in the Scriptures: Proverbs 3:26 says, "For the LORD shall be thy confidence, and shall keep thy foot from being taken." He won't let you fall. Psalm 37:24 says, "Though he fall, he shall not be utterly cast down: for the LORD upholdeth him with his hand." In 1 Samuel 2:9 Hannah said, "He will keep the feet of his saints. . . ." One of the last benedictions in the Bible occurs in the little epistle of Jude. "Now unto him that is able to keep you from falling [stumbling], and to present you faultless before the presence of his glory with exceeding joy, To the only wise God our Saviour, be now and ever. Amen" (Jude 24–25). He is able to keep us. He is the keeper of Israel and the keeper of His own today.

Notice that He keeps us both day and night. He doesn't slumber or sleep. When they camped for the night and were sleeping in a strange country, God didn't sleep—He was still watching over them.

"The sun shall not smite thee by day, nor the moon by night." They traveled at certain seasons when the sun was really hot—I know how hot that sun can be over there. But He said He would keep them in the scorching heat. But what about "the moon by night"? Well, I don't know exactly what is meant by that. However, I do know that the word lunatic comes from the Latin word for moon—luna, and it arose from the widespread belief that the rays of the moon affect the minds of men. I can remember that when I was young I used to take a girl out on a date and the moonlight had an effect on us. But God can keep you— He can keep you in the sunshine and the moonlight. "The LORD shall preserve thy going out and thy coming in from this time forth, and even for evermore."

PSALM 122

This is the third song of degrees. In Psalm 120 we saw the Jew in distress; he was in a neighborhood that was unfavorable to him— he was being talked about and lied about. He leaves that, takes his family, and goes up to Jerusalem to celebrate one of the feasts of the Jews. In Psalm 121 he comes within sight of the Judean hills. He continues traveling until he reaches the wonderful city of Jerusalem. This is where the tribes come to celebrate the feasts of the Lord.

> **I was glad when they said unto me, Let us go into the house of the Lord.**
>
> **Our feet shall stand within thy gates, O Jerusalem.**
>
> **Jerusalem is builded as a city that is compact together:**
>
> **Whither the tribes go up, the tribes of the Lord, unto the testimony of Israel, to give thanks unto the name of the Lord [Ps. 122:1–4].**

The weary pilgrims after their long journey stand at last in the gates of their beloved Jerusalem. They lift their eyes to the temple—there it stands with its shining gold glittering in the bright sunlight. A glad cry passes from lip to lip, "Let us go into the house of the Lord!"

This beautiful psalm is also a prophecy. It is a millennial psalm looking forward to the time when all the tribes will go up to Jerusalem and assemble themselves for worship.

They have been out of their city for a long time. They actually do not have full possession of it today. They cannot build their temple on the temple site because the Mosque of Omar is there. All of the sacred places are pretty well covered by Gentiles. In Hosea 3:4–5 we read, "For the children of Israel shall abide many days without a king, and without a prince, and without a sacrifice, and without an image, and without an ephod, and without teraphim: Afterward shall the children of Israel return, and seek the LORD their God, and David their king; and shall fear the LORD and his goodness in the latter days."

There is going to be a millennial Jerusalem. And what will the returning tribes find? Dr. Gaebelein describes it this way: "A magnificent city compacted together, not only architecturally, a vast, a great, a beautiful city, but compacted together spiritually. Her warfare is over. She is no longer in strife and in danger of attack" (*The Book of Psalms*, p. 447). This will be the city of Jerusalem in the Millennium.

What a glorious prospect this psalm pictures!

PSALMS 123—125

THEME: The pilgrims see the temple, then Mount Zion, and finally stand in the security of Jerusalem

These are also a part of the pilgrim psalms and form a little cluster of three psalms that tell a story. Psalm 123 has been called "the eye of hope" because the temple comes into view, and the children of Israel turn their eyes to God in hope. The temple was a means of approach to God.

> **Unto thee lift I up mine eyes, O thou that dwellest in the heavens [Ps. 123:1].**

The psalmist is making it very clear that God is not confined to the temple; He is not in a "box" in Jerusalem. The critic is wrong when he says that Israel considered Jehovah God a local deity who lived in their little temple in Jerusalem. The psalmist makes it abundantly clear that Israel did not believe any such thing. He addresses Him: "O thou that dwellest in the heavens." The pilgrim comes within sight of the temple, but it causes him to lift his eyes to heaven, knowing that God dwelt in the heavens. The temple was only a means of approach to God.

> **Behold, as the eyes of servants look unto the hand of their masters, and as the eyes of a maiden unto the hand of her mistress; so our eyes wait upon the LORD our God, until that he have mercy upon us [Ps. 123:2].**

When you are working for someone, you watch the clock and you watch the boss. You are sure to be working when he is watching you. How many of us live as though God is looking at us all the time? Well, He is. We are always under His eye.

Have mercy upon us, O Lord, have mercy upon us: for
we are exceedingly filled with contempt [Ps. 123:3].

The children of Israel have been despised in the world, and now they
are coming to Jerusalem. They are asking for mercy, knowing they are
sinners and need God's mercy. They have not come to Jerusalem to pat
themselves on the back.

Our soul is exceedingly filled with the scorning of those
that are at ease, and with the contempt of the proud [Ps.
123:4].

Israel has now come to Jerusalem—the eye of hope. They are looking to
the One who dwells in the heavens. I wonder if we are looking in that
direction today?

Psalm 124 is a historical psalm. And Psalm 123 is the "eye of
hope" looking to the future, so Psalm 124 is the eye of the past, review-
ing the history of God's mercy to them in the past.

If it had not been the Lord who was on our side, now
may Israel say:

If it had not been the Lord who was on our side, when
men rose up against us:

Then they had swallowed us up quick, when their wrath
was kindled against us [Ps. 124:1–3].

As the Israelites look back over their history, it is obvious that God has
moved in their lives and made it possible for them to go up to Jerusalem to worship. For this they are giving thanks to God.

Then the waters had overwhelmed us, the stream had
gone over our soul [Ps. 124:4].

These would be the waters of the Red Sea and the waters of the Jordan
River and the waters of circumstances in which they found themselves
many times.

> **Blessed be the LORD, who hath not given us as a prey to their teeth [Ps. 124:6].**

They know it is God who has helped them.

> **Our help is in the name of the LORD, who made heaven and earth [Ps. 124:8].**

The children of Israel are worshiping the Creator, "who made heaven and earth." This is a wonderful little psalm.

Now in Psalm 125, as the pilgrim sees Mount Zion, his heart is encouraged for the future. For our own hearts we can bring this up to date and say, "Being confident of this very thing, that he which hath begun a good work in you will perform it until the day of Jesus Christ" (Phil. 1:6). This has been called a "Song of Security" and is a prediction of Israel's national restoration.

> **They that trust in the LORD shall be as mount Zion, which cannot be removed, but abideth for ever [Ps. 125:1].**

The pilgrims have come from all over the land and beyond the land. As they came they saw the mountains of Judea. Then they saw the hills around Jerusalem, and now they can actually see Mount Zion. They are moving toward Jerusalem and can see the city clearly.

> **As the mountains are round about Jerusalem, so the LORD is round about his people from henceforth even for ever [Ps. 125:2].**

This is a wonderful psalm with blessed assurance that all who put their trust in Jehovah are like the unmovable, never-changing Mount Zion.

PSALM 126

THEME: A song of joy after their return from Babylonian captivity

When the Lord turned again to the captivity of Zion, we were like them that dream [Ps. 126:1].

It seemed too good to be true that they were able to return to Jerusalem. It was like a dream—they couldn't believe it.

Then was our mouth filled with laughter, and our tongue with singing: then said they among the heathen, The Lord hath done great things for them [Ps. 126:2].

Now they want to give a testimony to the world.

The Lord hath done great things for us; whereof we are glad [Ps. 126:3].

The remnant of Israel that returned to their land after the Babylonian captivity does not exhaust the meaning of this psalm. It also looks forward to their national restoration when their Messiah, the Lord Jesus Christ, returns.

Turn again our captivity, O Lord, as the streams in the south.

They that sow in tears shall reap in joy.

He that goeth forth and weepeth, bearing precious seed, shall doubtless come again with rejoicing, bringing his sheaves with him [Ps. 126:4-6].

Let me quote Dr. Gaebelein's comment at the conclusion of this psalm. "Beautiful is the ending of this Psalm of prophecy. We must think first of all of Him who came in humility and sowed His precious seed with tears, our Lord Jesus Christ. . . . Only His Father knows the many tears which He shed in His presence in secret prayer. . . . And it is perfectly proper to apply this to ourselves also. So let us weep and scatter the seed! 'Let us not be weary in well-doing; for in due season we shall reap, if we faint not' " (*The Book of Psalms,* p. 456).

PSALM 127

THEME: The vanity of building without God

This is another great pilgrim psalm. It has been called "The Cotter's Saturday Night Song," which is probably as good as any name. It is a mighty crescendo. Here you come to the crest of the psalms. We are at the highest elevation when we reach the temple area and Mount Zion in Jerusalem, but his psalm carries us right into the heavenlies. This is a psalm that is applicable to us in our day, and it reveals an utter dependence upon God.

This psalm has been used on several important occasions. It was used at the inauguration of President Eisenhower. Two Bibles were used. One of them was George Washington's Bible, and it was opened at Psalm 127.

The inscription "A Song of degrees for Solomon" does not appear in the Septuagint Version. There are those who hold that the expression "my beloved" refers to Solomon, but the son of David mentioned here is not Solomon; He is none other than the Lord Jesus Christ Himself.

> Except the LORD build the house, they labour in vain that build it: except the LORD keep the city, the watchman waketh but in vain.
>
> It is vain for you to rise up early, to sit up late, to eat the bread of sorrows: for so he giveth his beloved sleep [Ps. 127:1–2].

The word *vain* is used three times in these verses. My friend, everything is vain unless God is in it. Everything is dependent on Him and on His blessings. An old German proverb says, "Everything depends on the blessing of God." I wish we looked at things like that. This is why this psalm has been called "The Cotter's Saturday Night Song."

The Lord Jesus Christ said, "Therefore take no thought, saying, What shall we eat? or, What shall we drink? or, Wherewithal shall we be clothed? (For after all these things do the Gentiles seek:) for your heavenly Father knoweth that ye have need of all these things. But seek ye first the kingdom of God, and his righteousness; and all these things shall be added unto you. Take therefore no thought for the morrow: for the morrow shall take thought for the things of itself. Sufficient unto the day is the evil thereof" (Matt. 6:31–34).

In this psalm we find a reference to children. When the pilgrim went to Jerusalem, he took his family to worship with him.

> **Lo, children are an heritage of the LORD: and the fruit of the womb is his reward [Ps. 127:3].**

Here is the pilgrim, his wife, and his children, all of them are in Jerusalem to thank God.

> **As arrows are in the hand of a mighty man; so are children of the youth.**

> **Happy is the man that hath his quiver full of them: they shall not be ashamed, but they shall speak with the enemies in the gate [Ps. 127:4–5].**

His children will defend him. It is a comforting thing to have a child who will defend you and to have a whole little army of them is quite wonderful. The psalmist who wrote this knew nothing about the population explosion.

PSALM 128

Luther called this a "Marriage Song." It describes a happy family life and then gives the invocation of the Lord's blessing. It is God's picture of a happy family, and notice its foundation:

> **Blessed is every one that feareth the Lord; that walketh in his ways [Ps. 128:1].**

What is it that makes a family happy? What foundation must be laid? There are all kinds of conferences for the family, especially the young family. They are to adopt certain methods and adjust themselves to certain procedures. My friend, you can never have a happy home until the fear of the Lord is in that home, until the members of the family walk day by day in the ways of the Lord. This idea of working things out psychologically simply will not work. It reminds me of the man who, when asked how he had lived so long, said it was because he had lived an outdoor life. He explained that when he and his wife got married they decided that every time they had a quarrel he would go outside. So, he said, "I have lived an outdoor life." Well, my friend, that is not the solution. There must be the fear of the Lord in the home.

> **For thou shalt eat the labour of thine hands: happy shalt thou be, and it shall be well with thee [Ps. 128:2].**

The husband works and provides for his family.

> **Thy wife shall be as a fruitful vine by the sides of thine house: thy children like olive plants round about thy table [Ps. 128:3].**

If there is a family altar, this is it. I do not like the present set-up of many family altars where it is a hit-and-miss proposition. The family comes together in a hurry, a few verses of Scripture are read, and then everyone starts out in a different direction. They are like the cowboy who mounted his horse and rode off in every direction. That seems to be the way the family altar is conducted in many instances. In this passage the husband, wife, and children gather about the table.

Behold, that thus shall the man be blessed that feareth the LORD [Ps. 128:4].

You cannot get away from the fact that, unless there is that reverential fear of God and obedience to Him, there will not be a happy home. Children know if their parents love the Lord, and if they serve Him, and if they obey Him, and if He is important in their lives. There is no substitute for the godly life. You can go to all of the conferences you want to, but you will never have a happy home until your relationship with God is right. When you get rightly related to God, it will amaze you how many of your problems will fall into place and take care of themselves.

The LORD shall bless thee out of Zion: and thou shalt see the good of Jerusalem all the days of thy life.

Yea, thou shalt see thy children's children, and peace upon Israel [Ps. 128:5–6].

An interesting statement has been made in reference to this psalm, and I would like to pass it on to you. It says, "Before the fall, paradise was man's home. After the fall, the home was man's paradise." Home can be either paradise or the exact opposite of it.

This is a wonderful little family psalm.

PSALMS 129 AND 130

THEME: Burned but not consumed

In Psalm 129 the pilgrim reviews his youth and the hand of God upon him. It is also a picture of Israel burned but not consumed. The burning bush seen by Moses is the emblem of the miraculous preservation of God's people. What a picture we have here!

God has delivered the pilgrims, and they are in Jerusalem to worship.

> **Many a time have they afflicted me from my youth, may Israel now say:**
>
> **Many a time have they afflicted me from my youth: yet they have not prevailed against me [Ps. 129:1–2].**

Israel was not destroyed because God had preserved them.

> **Neither do they which go by say, The blessing of the Lord be upon you: we bless you in the name of the Lord [Ps. 129:8].**

"The blessing of the Lord be upon you" should be incorporated not only into the home but also into business today. A man's religion and his right relationship to God should be an integral part of both his home life and his business life. Boaz was a businessman. When he spoke to his workers, he said to them, ". . . The Lord be with you. And they answered him, The Lord bless thee" (Ruth 2:4). You don't find capital and labor talking like that to each other today.

Psalm 130 is closely linked to the preceeding psalm. It has been called a Pauline psalm because it speaks of that which has to do with the mercy of God. God has delivered man out of the depths of sin and death, and He has done it not on the basis of man's works. On a certain occasion Martin Luther was asked what were the best psalms. He answered by saying "Psalmi Paulini," the Pauline psalms. When they wanted to know what the Pauline psalms were, he replied, "The thirty-second, the fifty-first, the one hundred and thirtieth, and the one hundred and forty-third." He explained that these psalms teach us that the forgiveness of sins is vouchsafed to all who believe without having any works of the law to offer. Therefore, they are Pauline psalms.

This psalm has been inscribed "De Profundis"—out of the depths.

> **Out of the depths have I cried unto thee, O Lord.**
>
> **Lord, hear my voice: let thine ears be attentive to the voice of my supplications.**
>
> **If thou, Lord, shouldest mark iniquities, O Lord, who shall stand? [Ps. 130:1–3].**

Thank God that He is not going to judge us according to our iniquities. If God judged us that way, we would all be lost. It is because of His mercy that He saves us.

> **But there is forgiveness with thee, that thou mayest be feared.**
>
> **I wait for the Lord, my soul doth wait, and in his word do I hope.**
>
> **My soul waiteth for the Lord more than they that watch for the morning: I say, more than they that watch for the morning [Ps. 130:4–6].**

The grace that saves us as Gentiles will save the nation of Israel also. The day is coming when Israel's cry out of the depths will be answered. Christ will return unto Zion and will turn away ungodliness from Jacob: "And so all Israel shall be saved: as it is written, There shall come out of Sion the Deliverer, and shall turn away ungodliness from Jacob: For this is my covenant unto them, when I shall take away their sins. As concerning the gospel, they are enemies for your sakes: but as touching the election, they are beloved for the fathers' sakes" (Rom. 11:26–28). During the Great Tribulation they will wait for the Lord to deliver them more than the watchers for the morning. You and I also are to wait for the rising of the Bright and Morning Star, the Lord Jesus Christ, when He comes for His own.

PSALM 131

THEME: Childlike faith and simplicity of the pilgrim

This is another pilgrim psalm, a brief but very precious one. Notice that it is written by David.

> LORD, my heart is not haughty, nor mine eyes lofty: neither do I exercise myself in great matters, or in things too high for me [Ps. 131:1].

Do you remember Michal who was David's wife and Saul's daughter? She despised David and mocked him because of the way he took the ark into the tabernacle (2 Sam. 6:12–23). David told his wife that he would probably be even more contemptible in her eyes, because he was going to humble himself even more and get down in the dust before his God. Remember, he was king. We need to get down before our God today. When was the last time you got down on all fours before God? Very few of us practice that. It is the best exercise there is. It certainly will help you spiritually, and it may help you physically.

> Surely I have behaved and quieted myself, as a child that is weaned of his mother: my soul is even as a weaned child.

> Let Israel hope in the LORD from henceforth and for ever [Ps. 131:2–3].

Let me quote Dr. Gaebelein's comment on this beautiful psalm: "Here we find the description of an humble, a broken and contrite spirit. It has well been said, 'All virtues together are a body of which humility is the head.' How many Scriptures teach the great importance and value of such true humility" (*The Book of Psalms*, p. 462). Then he cites several references in Scripture: "Though the LORD be high, yet hath he respect unto the lowly: but the proud he knoweth afar off" (Ps. 138:6). "For thus saith the high and lofty One that inhabiteth eternity, whose name is Holy; I dwell in the high and holy place, with him also that is of a contrite and humble spirit, to revive the spirit of the humble, and to revive the heart of the contrite ones" (Isa. 57:15). "Likewise, ye younger, submit yourselves unto the elder. Yea, all of you be subject one to another, and be clothed with humility: for God resisteth the proud, and giveth grace to the humble" (1 Pet. 5:5). "But let it be the hidden man of the heart, in that which is not corruptible, even the ornament of a meek and quiet spirit, which is in the sight of God of great price" (1 Pet. 3:4). "Humble yourselves in the sight of the Lord, and he shall lift you up" (James 4:10). And the Lord Jesus Himself said, "Come unto me, all ye that labour and are heavy laden, and I will give you rest [literally, I will rest you]" (Matt. 11:28).

The figure of a weaned child is very interesting. Dr. Gaebelein comments, "As the weaned child no longer cries, and frets, and longs for the mother's breast, but rests still and is contented, because the child knows it is with its mother; so the soul is weaned from all discontentment, ambitiousness and selfseeking, or any kind of selfishness, waiting on the Lord, finding rest and contentment only in Him" (ibid., p. 463).

PSALM 132

THEME: A messianic psalm looking forward to the time Christ will be King in Jerusalem

This is another pilgrim psalm that speaks of a rest on the promises of God, and faith becomes all important. There has always been a question about the authorship of this psalm. David is mentioned four times, but I do not believe he wrote it. Those of real scholarship question that David wrote it. Delitzsch says, "It is suited to the mouth of Solomon." Perowne says, "It is perfectly natural that Solomon should write a song for such an occasion, speaking of the earlier efforts made by his father to prepare a habitation for Jehovah." It is his belief that this psalm was composed by King Solomon when the ark of the covenant was removed out of the tent of habitation that David had prepared for it in Jerusalem, and which was now being moved into the temple that Solomon had built. This idea seems to fit in better with the contents of this psalm, and the only mention we have of the ark in the Psalms is here.

We need to note, however, that the son of David in this psalm is not Solomon, but the greater Son of David, the Lord Jesus Christ. With this as a background, let us look at this psalm. Now that the pilgrims are there in Jerusalem, they have come to the temple where the mercy seat is above the ark, the place where they can approach God.

LORD, remember David, and all his afflictions:

How he sware unto the LORD, and vowed unto the mighty God of Jacob;

Surely I will not come into the tabernacle of my house, nor go up into my bed;

I will not give sleep to mine eyes, or slumber to mine eyelids.

> **Until I find out a place for the LORD, an habitation for the
> mighty God of Jacob [Ps. 132:1–5].**

You will recall that in 2 Samuel 7 it was in David's heart to build God a
house. You can see from this passage that this was the overwhelming
ambition of his life. His one great, pulsating thought was that he might
build a temple for the ark of God.

> **Arise, O LORD, into thy rest; thou, and the ark of thy
> strength [Ps. 132:8].**

This evidently was the song that they sang when the ark was moved
into the temple that Solomon had built, and the glory of the Lord filled
the temple as it had the tabernacle of old.

> **The LORD hath sworn in truth unto David: he will not
> turn from it; Of the fruit of thy body will I set upon thy
> throne [Ps. 132:11].**

This is a reference to the Lord Jesus Christ. Can we be sure of this? Yes,
because David's children did not measure up to the description of the
One who one day would sit upon the throne of David. In the Books of
Kings and Chronicles you follow the line of David, and you will see
one sinner after another sitting upon the throne. Very few were good
kings, and only five of them saw revival come to the nation.

> **If thy children will keep my covenant and my testimony
> that I shall teach them, their children shall also sit upon
> thy throne for evermore [Ps. 132:12].**

But, you see, David's children did not keep God's covenant and testimony. That is the reason they were put out of their land and sent into
captivity in Babylon. Even though the line of David sinned, God's covenant was not destroyed, and the time will come when the fruit of his
body will sit upon his throne. That is what the New Testament speaks
about when it opens with, "The book of the generation of Jesus Christ,

the son of David, the son of Abraham" (Matt. 1:1). The Lord Jesus is the "Son of David" that the psalmist is writing about.

> **For the LORD hath chosen Zion; he hath desired it for his habitation.**
>
> **This is my rest for ever: here will I dwell; for I have desired it.**
>
> **I will abundantly bless her provision: I will satisfy her poor with bread [Ps. 132:13–15].**

This prophecy is not fulfilled in Jerusalem in our day. I walked up on top of Mount Zion one day with a friend, and when he saw what was there, he said, "I wonder if it was worth the walk?" I told him, "I guess David and the Lord thought so, but there is something in the future that they can see and we do not see."

It is apparent that this is a psalm that the pilgrims would sing as they came to Jerusalem and the temple where God promised He would meet with His people.

PSALM 133

THEME: Rejoicing in the fellowship of believers

This psalm is "A Song of degrees of David." It is short, but it is a beautiful gem. It has been called "A Psalm of Brotherhood," and it certainly is a psalm of fellowship. Not only did this pilgrim come to Jerusalem with his wife and children, but he is with friends. They are having a wonderful time of fellowship together. Remember that these pilgrims came from all over the then-known world, and they had been suffering persecution among unbelievers. What a joyful experience it is for them to be with their own people who are worshiping God with them.

> **Behold, how good and how pleasant it is for brethren to dwell together in unity! [Ps. 133:1].**

As believers, we are told to endeavor to ". . . keep the unity of the Spirit in the bond of peace" (Eph. 4:3). Believers are one in Christ. My friend, let's avoid being in a little exclusive clique. Unfortunately, we have a lot of cliques in our churches today. Many people would rather be big fish in little ponds than little fish in big ponds. How much better it is for all believers to "dwell together in unity!"

> **It is like the precious ointment upon the head, that ran down upon the beard, even Aaron's beard: that went down to the skirts of his garments [Ps. 133:2].**

This verse refers to the time that Aaron was anointed high priest. It also speaks of the priesthood of the Lord Jesus Christ. Someone has said that in this verse you have the fragrance of a lovely rose. This precious ointment was put on the priest to indicate that he was a priest unto God. We see that this is a picture of the Lord Jesus Christ. Not only is He King; He is also our High Priest. It is said of Him in Psalm

45:7 that He is anointed ". . . with the oil of gladness above [His] fol lows." In Ezekiel 39:29 we read, "Neither will I hide my face any more from them: for I have poured out my spirit upon the house of Israel, saith the Lord God." Ezekiel speaks of a future day, and like that ointment that ran down on Aaron, so will God pour out His Spirit. This is the meaning, by the way, of Joel's prophecy of the outpouring of the Holy Spirit upon the Israel of a coming day, which was not fulfilled on the day of Pentecost. However, in our day we are baptized with the Holy Spirit, which puts us in the body of believers; and Christ is our Great High Priest. Since this is true, we should attempt to keep the unity the Holy Spirit made.

The psalmist concludes by saying that for brethren to dwell together in unity is—

As the dew of Hermon, and as the dew that descended upon the mountains of Zion: for there the Lord commanded the blessing, even life for evermore [Ps. 133:3].

This psalm is a beautiful little gem.

PSALM 134

THEME: The pilgrim's final song of praise

This is the final psalm in the pilgrim's progress. We have arrived. And in this psalm the pilgrim stands in the temple and lifts his voice in praise with the multitude. This is the grand amen, a threefold amen.

> **Behold, bless ye the LORD, all ye servants of the LORD, which by night stand in the house of the LORD.**
>
> **Lift up your hands in the sanctuary, and bless the LORD [Ps. 134:1–2].**

Again I remind you that this pilgrim had come from a place where he was under suspicion. People criticized him, maligned him, and lied about him. His neighborhood was not good. But now he has arrived in Jerusalem; he is standing in the sanctuary lifting up his hands and blessing the Lord.

> **The LORD that made heaven and earth bless thee out of Zion [Ps. 134:3].**

The pilgrim blesses God and, in turn, he is looking for the blessing of God to be upon his life. This is a great worship psalm and one that should be incorporated into our worship.

Let me venture a suggestion. The curse of being a retired preacher is that you always want to tell the other fellow how to conduct his service—whether you did it like that yourself or not. I know something about retired preachers, because several of them used to be in my congregations. Now I find myself one of them. As I look back on my ministry I realize my services were too formal. I believe worship today is entirely too formal. I do not believe that there should be fanatical outbreaks during the worship services, but there are some of us who cannot sing to express our thoughts. I have to stand in services just like a dummy. I can't sing—I can't carry a tune. My wife doesn't want me even to try to sing when I am standing with her in a service. She tells me that everybody turns and looks at me with not very pleasant looks when I try to sing. Sometimes I would just like to say, "Praise the Lord—Hallelujah" or "How wonderful is our God. God is good." We need some informality in our services and the freedom to express ourselves. Oh, my friend, let's not be stiff and stilted when we worship our God. Let's praise Him from our hearts.

PSALM 135

THEME: Praise the Lord

We leave the pilgrim psalms now and come to songs of praise. This is a hallelujah psalm. It begins with "Praise ye the LORD," and it ends with "Praise ye the LORD." This psalm is in a parentheses of "Hallelujahs." In it Israel praises God for the deliverance of the past. It is a great call to praise God.

> **Praise ye the LORD. Praise ye the name of the LORD; praise him, O ye servants of the LORD.**
>
> **Ye that stand in the house of the LORD, in the courts of the house of our God.**
>
> **Praise the LORD; for the LORD is good: sing praises unto his name; for it is pleasant [Ps. 135:1–3].**

We do not say enough that God is good. My friend, have you told anyone today that God is good? Oh, He *is* good! This is a call to praise Him.

> **Whatsoever the LORD pleased, that did he in heaven, and in earth, in the seas, and all deep places.**
>
> **He causeth the vapours to ascend from the ends of the earth; he maketh lightnings for the rain; he bringeth the wind out of his treasuries [Ps. 135:6–7].**

It is God who makes the weather. The weatherman does not make the weather, and the proof is that he does not always give us the correct report. He is not in touch with headquarters. He is in touch with a lot of scientific gadgets, and every now and then he comes up with an educated guess; but *God* makes the weather. He is the Creator. Not only does He make the weather, but He runs the universe as it pleases Him.

Maybe you don't like it; if you don't, why don't you move out? Why don't you go to another universe or start one of your own and run it your way? This is God's universe, and if you are not satisfied with it, I suggest that somehow you become reconciled to it and accept the Creator because He is also the Redeemer of man today. We have many questions that God has not answered. And frankly, my friend, God does not have to answer our questions. He asks us to trust Him and live a life of faith.

The psalmist compares the living God with idols.

> **The idols of the heathen are silver and gold, the work of men's hands.**
>
> **They have mouths, but they speak not; eyes have they, but they see not;**
>
> **They have ears, but they hear not; neither is there any breath in their mouths.**
>
> **They that make them are like unto them: so is every one that trusteth in them [Ps. 135:15–18].**

My friend, you are going to be like your god. What do you worship? You worship something. It could be gold or silver; it doesn't have to be in the shape of an image or an idol either. Many people today worship gold and silver. That is covetousness and modern idolatry. Whatever your god is—if it is not the living and true God—he may have a mouth, but he cannot speak. He may have ears, but he cannot hear you. Only the living God can hear you. Because you will become like your god, it is a good idea to worship the true God. We ought to bless His name.

> **Blessed be the LORD out of Zion, which dwelleth at Jerusalem. Praise ye the LORD [Ps. 135:21].**

He is worthy to be praised. This is a tremendous psalm!

PSALM 136

THEME: *Thanks to God for His mercy*

This is another hallelujah psalm. It praises God's mercy in creation, in redemption, in fighting enemies, and for the future glory.

> **O give thanks unto the LORD; for he is good: for his mercy endureth for ever [Ps. 136:1].**

The Lord has plenty of mercy. He will never run out of it.

> **O give thanks unto the God of gods: for his mercy endureth for ever.**

> **O give thanks to the Lord of lords: for his mercy endureth for ever [Ps. 136:2–3].**

Every verse in this psalm mentions the mercy of God. It exalts God's mercy. In Ephesians 2:4 Paul says, "But God, who is rich in mercy, for his great love wherewith he loved us." I want mercy from God, and He is rich in it. I receive many letters from folks who tell me they have committed some sin. They ask, "Do you think God will forgive me?" Friend, He is rich in mercy. Have you called on Him? If you really want forgiveness, He will give it to you. He deals with us according to His mercy.

This is praise to God the Creator. And notice that every verse has the refrain: "for his mercy endureth for ever."

> **To him that by wisdom made the heavens: for his mercy endureth for ever.**

> **To him that stretched out the earth above the waters: for his mercy endureth for ever.**

> **To him that made great lights: for his mercy endureth for ever:**

> The sun to rule by day: for his mercy endureth for ever:
>
> The moon and stars to rule by night: for his mercy endureth for ever [Ps. 136:5–9].

The next section is praise to God for His mercy in delivering Israel from Egyptian bondage. And with every step of God's deliverance He repeats: "for his mercy endureth for ever." He concludes with God's mercy in giving them their land:

> And gave their land for an heritage: for his mercy endureth for ever:
>
> Even an heritage unto Israel his servant: for his mercy endureth for ever [Ps. 136:21–22].

The concluding section of this glorious psalm is as meaningful to you and me as it is to the people of Israel:

> Who remembered us in our low estate: for his mercy endureth for ever:
>
> And hath redeemed us from our enemies: for his mercy endureth for ever.
>
> Who giveth food to all flesh: for his mercy endureth for ever.
>
> O give thanks unto the God of heaven: for his mercy endureth for ever [Ps. 136:23–26].

I don't know about you, but I feel like saying "Hallelujah" again. How wonderful is our God! Learn to fall down before Him and worship Him. He is worthy. When you get down in the dust (and you have to get down to get up), He will lift you up with His mercy.

PSALM 137

THEME: Singing the Lord's song in a strange land

Reading through the Book of Psalms is like driving on a divided highway through some lovely section of the countryside. We pass through new and beautiful scenery with a spectacular landscape on each side.

The beginning of each psalm is like coming to an intersection. We casually observe the highway marker, but we proceed at the same speed, and we have the feeling of sameness. On each side of the highway marker the view is very much the same. That is true especially after we leave Psalm 119. As we are traveling along the highway, all of a sudden we come to Psalm 137. When we come to this psalm we begin to slow down because we see down the highway that three flares have been thrown down. In fact, these three flares are telling us to Stop—Look—Listen.

By way of introduction, will you note these three flares. The first one is marked STOP.

As we come to this psalm we find that it is designated an imprecatory psalm. Somebody says, "Well, a flare with that word on it wouldn't make me stop because I wouldn't know what it meant anyway." May I say to you that *imprecatory* simply means that it is a psalm that pronounces a curse. It is a psalm that voices a prayer or a wish for vengeance. Listen to this concluding verse: "Happy shall he be, that taketh and dasheth thy little ones against the stones"! That is a red flare, let me tell you! It is a shocker, and it causes a great deal of difficulty. Many folk detour around it. In fact, it would be very easy for me to avoid it, but I feel that this psalm is one that we should stop and look at.

There are several ways men have of dealing with this psalm. The liberal critics deal with it very simply: they reject it. They say that it does not belong in the Bible. It expresses feelings that are contrary to what they think it ought to say. Therefore they reject it. Of course, the method of the higher critic is to take out of the Bible what he likes and reject what he does not like. He is like the simpleminded country boy who bought a cow. After he had bought the cow he learned it cost something to feed the front end of the cow, but he got the milk from the back end of the cow. He decided to concentrate on the back end, and forget about the front end so he could make more money. You know what happened—his cow died. But he was a "higher critic." Higher critics take what they like and reject what they do not like. This philosophy does not satisfy, nor does it solve the problem at all.

Then there is another way of dealing with this. There are those who say, in a naive sort of way, "I believe the Bible from cover to cover"—yet they are ignorant of what is between the covers! This is the reason those of us who are conservative are accused of being anti-intellectual. Multitudes of conservative folk claim to believe the Bible but are ignorant of it. This is the reason I put such an emphasis on teaching the Word of God. It is one thing to say you believe; it is another thing to know what it says.

This leads us to the third viewpoint. It is to believe the Bible from cover to cover, and attempt to understand it. It is to determine what God's meaning is, to discover what He had in mind when He recorded certain things. I want to know what I am believing, and be able to give a reason for the hope that is in me. Therefore with this attitude let us come to Psalm 137, an imprecatory psalm. Although it expresses something here that sounds very terrible on the surface, let's look at it and see what it really says.

The second flare tells us not only to stop, but to LOOK. That is, Psalm 137 deals with a particular portion of the history of God's chosen people. It is an historical psalm—which is very unusual. The historical books of the Old Testament do not record the history of the nation Israel during the seventy years of captivity in Babylon. There is no record of that captivity. It is true that Jeremiah prophesied about it, but he did not go with the captives to Babylon. Ezekiel was in Babylon, but he was prophesying to the captives there. We can only draw by inference the conditions of the people. He was concerned more with his visions than he was with history. Also Daniel was in Babylon during that period; but he was in the court, prophesying to the gentile rulers. We have no record from him at all concerning the captives. The seventy years of Babylonian captivity are a period of silence. It is a vacuum. It is a void as far as the historical books are concerned. The two Books of Kings and the two Books of Chronicles bring us right up to the Babylonian captivity and the destruction of Jerusalem. The next historical books, Ezra, Nehemiah, and Esther, pick up the story after the seventy-year captivity is over and the people are back in their land. The captivity in Babylon is passed over, because in God's plan His clock stops when His people are out of their land. For this reason we have no record of this period. This fact gives great emphasis to Psalm 137 because it is a bridge over the "Grand Canyon" of silence. It is like a vista point along the highway where you can pull off the road and look at scenery you have never seen before. We don't see very much, but we see something of this silent period.

Then the third flare that has been thrown down is LISTEN. It is a question that has been raised: "How shall we sing the LORD'S song in a strange land?" (Ps. 137:4). I'm not sure that this question can be answered for these people. I'm not sure today that it can be answered for you and me unless we are willing to meet certain conditions. How can we sing the Lord's song in a strange land?

Psalm 137 records the tragic yet tender experience of these people during the seventy years of captivity. You will find in this psalm bitter hatred and deep love. You will find a people that are overwhelmed and overpowered by their emotions. They feel very deeply about what is recorded here.

THE CENTRAL EXPERIENCE

Notice first of all the central experience of these people.

> **By the rivers of Babylon, there we sat down, yea, we wept, when we remembered Zion [Ps. 137:1].**

The location is all important—"by the rivers of Babylon." These people have had an experience that no other people have had. From the land of Goshen to the ghettos of Europe they have known what it is to be away from their homeland, to be in a strange land. They know what it is to go all the way from the brickyards of Egypt to Babylonian canals. They know what it is to spend time in slave labor camps. By the rivers of Babylon was one place where they were persecuted, where they performed slave labor, a place where they suffered. By the rivers of Babylon.

The question arises: What were they doing there? To begin with, they had no business being there. God had put them in the Promised Land, and God had promised to keep them there as His witnesses as long as they were true to Him. What are they doing by the rivers of *Babylon?*

The rivers of Babylon are, of course, the canals. I think it is well accepted today that these are the people that dug those canals off the Tigris and Euphrates rivers. Those canals threaded through that section to irrigate the land. These are the people who from sunup to sundown wearily dug through that dry desert terrain. "By the rivers of Babylon, there we sat down." What a picture of deep dejection. What a picture of despair. What a picture of dire desperation. "There we sat down." What else could they do? "Yea, we wept, when we remembered Zion." How woebegone can you get!

The Psalms are songs of praise. The Psalms express joy, wonderful faith, hope, and confidence. But not this psalm. This is the psalm in which they throw in the crying towel. "Yea, we wept, when we remembered Zion." This is no psalm of praise. This is a psalm of deep indigo, as blue as you can possibly get. "We wept, when we remembered Zion."

What a contrast between Jerusalem and Babylon! Jerusalem yonder in the hills, beautiful for situation. Babylon, down on a dry plain. The people are not there because they want to be there. They are there because their city has been destroyed. They are there because the Babylonians, a people stronger than they, had invaded their city, taken them captive, and herded them like animals, and put them on slave labor. Now they are homesick. "We wept, when we remembered Zion."

Why are they there? They are there because they have sinned. If you want the explanation from another weeping one of that period, turn to Jeremiah. He was a crybaby, but don't find fault with him because, you see, when God chose a man to pronounce His judgment upon them, He chose a man with a tender heart. It was Jeremiah who told them their city was to be destroyed. It was Jeremiah who said they were going into captivity. God didn't use a brutal man to give that brutal message. He didn't choose a harsh man to give a harsh message. He chose a man with the heart of a woman. Jeremiah says, "My eyes were a fountain of tears. This message broke my heart." God sent that kind of a man so they would know how He felt about it. Listen to him in Lamentations. "Jerusalem hath grievously sinned; therefore she is removed . . ." (Lam. 1:8). Why are these people down there on the banks of the canals in Babylon? They have grievously sinned. That is the reason they are there.

Now listen to them:

We hanged our harps upon the willows in the midst thereof [Ps. 137:2].

They have no heart for singing. They have quit singing now. They will not have a choir there. There won't be any song service there. They are wailing instead of singing. They have put their harps upon the willows; they won't be needing them anymore. They couldn't sing the songs of Zion by the rivers of Babylon! It was yonder at the temple in Jerusalem where they went to sing praises to God. Now by the rivers of Babylon they hanged up their harps. These instruments of praise they put on the willow trees—weeping willows.

Today there are multitudes of Christians who have put their harps on the weeping willow trees. They have lost their song. They have no harp, but they are harping just the same about this and that.

Christian friend, have you lost your song? Maybe you can remember the joy you had when you first came to Christ. Have you lost your song today?

THE CRITICAL EXPERIENCE

For there they that carried us away captive required of us a song; and they that wasted us required of us mirth, saying, Sing us one of the songs of Zion [Ps. 137:3].

Now the people of Babylon had heard about the singing in Israel. The Israelites were world famous—as we shall see in a moment—for a very definite reason. And when it was heard that they were being brought to the canals outside the city of Babylon, that they were colonized there and put in slave labor camps, the 'Tanner Bus' company started running a tour out there because people wanted to see them. You see, Israel was world famous because in Jerusalem there was a temple to the living and true God. When visitors came to Jerusalem they found a people, not worshiping an image, but serving the living God, approaching Him through redemption and forgiveness of sins, and singing praises unto Him. They had never seen anything like it. They had never heard anything like it. The news of it spread throughout the world. The Queen of Sheba came from the ends of the earth when she heard of it. She thought the report couldn't be true. During Israel's feast seasons the people would gather together in Jerusalem, and they would sing these psalms. Probably all of the psalms were set to music. David arranged a choir and an orchestra with hundreds of musicians. It is estimated that there were times when one hundred thousand people gathered in and around that temple singing praises unto God! To hear them was a sensational experience. But now the temple was burned, Jerusalem lay in rubble, and the people were doing slave labor in Babylon. Many travelers came to Babylon saying something like this: "I was in Jerusalem during a feast day those people had. They were there from all over the world. They gathered around their temple over one hundred thousand strong. When that sacrifice was burned and the smoke ascended, out from the throats of those people rose a psalm that lifted me off the ground into the heavens! I have never heard anything like it!" (These people have been musicians, whether you like it or not, through the centuries—all the way from David, the sweet psalmist of Israel, to Meyerbeer, Offenbach, Fritz Kreisler, Felix Mendelssohn, George Gershwin, Paul Whiteman, Irving Berlin and to the present crop.)

When these people met together and sang praises to God, the world heard about it. God intended the world to hear about it. Now that they were captives in Babylon, the Babylonians said, "We're going out there and listen to a concert!" When they got out there the Babylonians saw the harps hanging on the willow trees; they saw these people sitting in deep dejection—instead of singing they were weeping. And with a sneer they said to them, "Sing us a song of Zion. We've been hearing about you. We thought you people could *sing!*" They taunted and ridiculed them, "Heist us a tune. Let's hear it."

Listen to them.

How shall we sing the LORD's song in a strange land? [Ps. 137:4].

With a sob in their soul they said, "We've lost our song. You mock us when you tell us to sing you a song of Zion. Our Zion is back yonder in ashes and rubble and ruin. We can't sing anywhere but back there. How can we sing the Lord's song in a strange land?"

The interesting thing is that the Christian *is* to sing in a strange land. The people of Israel were not; they were perfectly right in refusing. To begin with, they *couldn't* sing. Neither did God ask them to sing where they were. They were to sing the songs of Zion *at* Zion. The child of God today is a pilgrim and stranger in this world. Centuries before this time the people of Israel were going through the wilderness, with slavery in Egypt behind them, on their way to the Promised Land. In the lead were the Levites carrying the ark, and they were singing. Immediately behind them came Judah, the tribe whose name means "praise." They went through the wilderness with praise on their lips. Today this is the way in which the child of God is to go through the wilderness of this world. Every Christian today should have a song in his heart. I don't say a song on his lips—David made it very clear that we're to make a joyful *noise* unto the Lord. It's best for some of us not to sing aloud. I don't sing in public; I sing privately for my own amusement, usually in the car alone. But we are to sing in a strange land. God has given us a song, the song of redemption.

Now there are reasons for people losing their song: First of all, there is the natural tendency. That is, the psychological factor. Psychologists tell us that some folk are sanguine in their nature. That is, they are smiling, joyful all the time regardless of the circumstances. Other people are the opposite. They are filled with melancholy. Some *races* are like that. The Scottish have a reputation of being the dour Scots. I do not know, but I think I must have enough Scottish blood to give me a pessimistic view of life. Conversely, the contribution the black race has made in our midst is that they are a happy race. Under all circumstances they have revealed that. I heard the story of the black woman who was so radiant, regardless of circumstances, that they asked her what was her secret. She said, "Well, when I works, I works hard. When I rest, I sits loose, and when I worries, I goes to sleep." Isn't it wonderful to have that kind of a nature that when you worry you go to sleep! But a great many folk today don't look joyful. Some of us don't feel like smiling all the time. We're not made that way.

The second factor is that discouragement and disappointment come to a great many Christians. Life buffets some people more than it buffets others. You know some Christians that seem to have more trouble than anyone else. Shakespeare calls it "the slings and arrows of outrageous fortune." Some people seem to get more of the slings and arrows of outrageous fortune. When I first came to Los Angeles, I went out and stood on a street corner, watching the faces of those who went by. Folk had come there from everywhere. They had come largely to improve their condition, for entertainment, and for relaxation. But you will see as many unhappy faces on the streets of Southern California as you will see any place in the world. As I watched, in the midst of the many unhappy faces, I saw the face of a woman that just stood out. I had never seen a face that had tragedy marked on it as hers did. I wondered about it. I was startled when the next Sunday morning I looked out at the faces in my congregation, and there she sat. I was even more startled when that morning after the benediction she came to me and said, "I must talk to you." And when she told her story I agreed that her face should have looked just as it did—the saddest face I have ever seen. The discouragements of life sometimes beat in upon even children of God, and they lose their song.

Then there is the third reason. Sometimes folk lose their song because of sin. You remember that David in his great confession, recorded in Psalm 51:12, cried, "Restore unto me the joy of thy salvation." David never did lose his salvation, but he certainly lost the joy of it. That is what he asked God to restore. And in Psalm 32 he spoke of that awful, oppressive period when his sin was unconfessed. He said that his bones ached and he could not sleep. What a picture!

It was said of the Lord Jesus Christ that He was a Man of Sorrows and acquainted with grief. But before you make Him out a sad person—for He was not—note that Isaiah makes it very clear that He bore our griefs and carried our sorrows (Isa. 53:4). When all the sorrow and all the grief of your sin and my sin was put upon Him, He was a Man of Sorrows. But He had none of His own, for He had no sin of His own. He was made sin for us, and He was made our sin offering, completely identified with your sin and mine.

Why are these people by the rivers of Babylon? I can answer it now. *They have sinned.* Why have they lost their song? They sinned, and sin will rob you of your song.

THE CROWNING EXPERIENCE

Notice now in conclusion the crowning experience of these people.

> If I forget thee, O Jerusalem, let my right hand forget her cunning.
>
> If I do not remember thee, let my tongue cleave to the roof of my mouth; if I prefer not Jerusalem above my chief joy [Ps. 137:5–6].

And under the taunting of that mob of curious Babylonians who said, "Come on, let's hear something," they said, "We can't sing." Then they made a pledge to God. They said, "O Jerusalem, if I ever forget you, may my tongue cleave to the roof of my mouth. I'll never, never, *never* forget Jerusalem."

This is the ray of hope that is here. This is repentance. This is a pledge of allegiance. This is saying, "We'll become obedient now to God, and we want back in the will of God. We want to go back to Jerusalem." This is their confession. "If I forget thee, O Jerusalem. . . ."

> Remember, O LORD, the children of Edom in the day of Jerusalem; who said, Rase it, rase it, even to the foundation thereof [Ps. 137:7].

Edom, their eternal enemy, was there at the time Jerusalem fell, and Edom got in the cheering section for Babylon. They got up there and shouted, "Tear it down! Destroy it! We want to get rid of that wicked city!" They remember that now—these people who had survived that experience—and what they are asking for is justice. It is a cry for justice.

Someone is going to say, "But that is not the Christian spirit." I grant you, it is not. But these people are under law; they are not under grace. They are under law that provided justice. We may have misunderstood our Lord when on the cross He said, "Father, forgive them; for they know not what they do . . ." (Luke 23:34). Do you think He is dismissing all of the sins of these people? If you do, you are wrong. All He is saying is, "Father, forgive them for this particular thing of crucifying Me. They don't know what they are doing here." That crime is not to be held against them, but they are still sinners. And they will have to come to God as sinners, as one of them did—Saul of Tarsus, who was probably there at the time. He had to come to Christ and receive forgiveness of sin.

Somebody may remark that Stephen when he died said, ". . . Lord, lay not this sin to their charge . . ." (Acts 7:60). That is true. Stephen is exhibiting the attitude believers should take. Paul expresses it: "Dearly beloved, avenge not yourselves, but rather give place unto wrath: for it is written, Vengeance is mine; I will repay, saith the Lord" (Rom. 12:19). What is the Christian spirit? The Christian spirit is this: avenge not yourself. Does that mean that nothing is to be done about it? No. God says this to you and me as Christians: "Have you been harmed or hurt? Don't you hit back. I want you to turn that over to Me. I'll handle it. Vengeance is mine; I will repay." God is saying that He will not let them get by with it. You see, when you and I take matters in our own hands, we are forsaking the walk of faith. What we are really saying is, "Lord, I can't trust You to handle this. I'll handle this one myself." In other words, we really want to hurt Him in return. But God is saying, "You walk by faith. Turn this matter over to Me. I'm the God of justice." My friend, justice must prevail. It has to prevail.

Someone still protests, "But this isn't like the New Testament." What do you mean it isn't like the New Testament? I read this in Revelation 6:9–10: "And when he had opened the fifth seal, I saw under the altar the souls of them that were slain for the word of God, and for the testimony which they had: And they cried with a loud voice, saying, How long, O Lord, holy and true, dost thou not judge and avenge our blood on them that dwell on the earth?" A cry for vengeance is not contrary, you see, to the New Testament. My friend, justice must prevail. Our God is just. Things must be made right.

How deeply do you feel about evil? Do you hate a mad dog that comes into the yard to bite one of your children? If you don't love your children, then you wouldn't mind even bringing the mad dog into your home and urging the children to pet him on the head. But if you love your children, you will hate that mad dog.

It is said of our Lord when He comes the next time: "Thou lovest righteousness, and hatest wickedness . . ." (Ps. 45:7). You can't love righteousness without hating wickedness. You can't love God without hating Satan. You can't love that which is right without hating that which is wrong. How deeply, really, do you feel about evil?

These captives, down by the river in Babylon, felt very deeply, and all they were asking for was that justice might prevail.

O daughter of Babylon, who art to be destroyed; happy shall he be, that rewardeth thee as thou hast served us [Ps. 137:8].

This is the law of retribution. It is still a principle for the child of God today. "Be not deceived; God is not mocked: for whatsoever a man soweth, that shall he also reap" (Gal. 6:7). He won't reap something else, but he will reap the identical thing that he sowed.

What these people are saying is, "O God, let that thing happen to them that happened to us—" the law of retribution. Our Lord said it: ". . . they that take the sword shall perish with the sword" (Matt. 26:52).

Now we come to the real difficulty.

Happy shall he be, that taketh and dasheth thy little ones against the stones [Ps. 137:9].

This Israelite, sitting yonder by the canals of Babylon, dejected, despondent, being jeered and taunted to sing, says, "I can't sing." His mind goes back to the destruction of his beloved city and of God's temple. He thinks again of what took place. He can see that Edomite in the cheering section, urging the Babylonians on. He sees how the Babylonians had destroyed his city. And then happened that frightful, awful thing. His wife was holding their precious little one. That great big brutal Babylonian soldier came to her, wrested the baby out of her arms, took it by the heels, and—with her screaming—hit its head across the rock, dashing its brains out! Remembering that, he says, "Because there is a just God in heaven, somebody will do that to the Babylonians."

Whether you and I like it or not, it is already a matter of history that Cyrus the Great through his general did exactly to the Babylonians what the Babylonians had done to the people of Jerusalem.

Is this psalm for the Dark Ages? Is it outmoded in this enlightened day? Has man grown more civilized and loving so that this psalm is no longer relevant?

Today on every continent strife is being fomented. And the most tragic casualties are the children. Man's inhumanity to man makes this psalm very up-to-date. And there is coming a day when all hell will break loose in this world. I thank God there is a God in heaven who is a God of justice and righteousness, and He is going to put an end to sin. Also I am thankful that He is a God of mercy, that He is not like men, but is merciful. The cross yonder reveals His love; it reveals His holiness. My Savior took upon Himself my sin. God so loved me that He gave His Son to die in my place, because He must judge sin.

Oh, today, in this day of grace He is merciful. But don't let it deceive you—He is also holy, and He is righteous. Those who will not receive the Savior, those who will spurn His grace, those who will turn their backs on His mercy, will be judged. He makes no apologies to us in the twentieth century for doing that, because He has been patient with us. He has been gracious so long.

Have you availed yourself of His mercy?

PSALM 138

THEME: A song of wholehearted praise

We come from Psalm 137, where we saw the harps hanging on the willow trees, to the psalm before us where the harps are again in the hands of the godly and are being used for the praise and worship of Jehovah. In the previous psalm the children of Israel were in captivity, down by the irrigation canals in Babylon. There they put their harps on the willow trees and wept when they remembered Zion. But in Psalm 138 we have a wonderful prophetic hymn of praise which looks into the future when the believing remnant will take up their harps again and sing praise unto God.

This is a psalm of David. Because there is a reference to the temple (which was not in existence in David's day), David's authorship has been questioned. Well, the word *temple* could be translated "tabernacle" just as easily; and I believe it is speaking of the tabernacle and the days of David. After all, in the inspired text it is inscribed as a psalm of David.

I will praise thee with my whole heart: before the gods will I sing praise unto thee [Ps. 138:1].

Let me give you Dr. Gaebelein's translation: "I will give thanks unto Thee with my whole heart, before the gods will I sing praises unto Thee."

Notice "I will praise thee with my whole heart." One of the things that impressed me on a visit to Jerusalem was seeing the Jews at the Wailing Wall (Israel has access to the wall again). I saw many of them standing there, some of them with a little book in their hands going through a ritual, some of them actually butting their heads against the wall, and some of them actually wailing, which touches the heart. But a great deal that I saw was just like ritualistic "churchianity"— nothing but lip service. However, in that future time when the Jews have been through the period of Jacob's trouble, the Great Tribulation, and have been delivered out of it, there will no longer be lip service. It will be real heart worship—"I will praise thee with my whole heart." My friend, you and I need to examine our own hearts to see how we are worshiping God. Do we worship Him with our whole heart? One of the things which impressed me about Horatius Bonar was what he said when he went to God to repent of the coldness, the indifference, and the sin in his life. He said, "Then I went back to God and repented of my repentance." His first confession was merely lip service, and he repented of that. I think some of us ought to go to God in prayer on Monday morning and ask Him to forgive us for going to church on Sunday. We should pray, "Lord, forgive me for going to church yesterday. I sang the hymns, but my heart wasn't in it. I prayed, but it was a mere formality. I listened to the Word of God, but it had no effect on me. I criticized the preacher and others who were there, but I did not criticize myself. God, forgive me for going to church like that." This would be a good thing for many of us to pray.

"Before the gods will I sing praise unto thee." Luther and Calvin explain that the "gods" were angels of God—I don't think they were that. Others think that he was talking about the idol of the nations, and certainly he could be referring to them. However, anything in your life that is in place of God or is between you and God, is your god. We saw this word gods back in Psalm 82:6, and there it referred to the judges, those who are in the place of God, that is, His representatives on earth. I have always been mindful of the fact that as a teacher, preacher, and minister of the Word of God, I have a responsibility to God. Someday I will have to answer to Him, because it is my job to make the Gospel clear. If those who know the Lord don't make the Gospel clear, who will? When I look back upon my ministry, I see much failure, and I have many regrets; but some day I will be able to look into the face of God and say, "Lord, I preached Your Word the best I could." That is a great comfort, because I have been His representative here on this earth. So, you see, when David said, "Before the gods will I sing praise unto thee," he could have meant several things, and we cannot be sure exactly what he had in mind.

I will worship toward the holy temple, and praise thy name for thy lovingkindness and for thy truth: for thou hast magnified thy word above all thy name [Ps. 138:2].

A better translation of the last part of this verse would be, "Thou hast magnified thy saying according to all thy name." In other words, God's Word is as good as He is. There is an old saying that a man is as good as his word. Well, God is as good as His Word. His character is behind what He has said. "Thou hast magnified thy saying in accordance with all thy name," or, "Thou hast fulfilled it in such a manner as to bring out all that Thy name implies." This is a very wonderful statement.

Though the LORD be high, yet hath he respect unto the lowly: but the proud he knoweth afar off [Ps. 138:6].

Dr. Gaebelein translates it, "For Jehovah is high, and regardeth the humble, but the proud He knoweth afar off." He is high and He is over all; yet He will condescend to the lowly. There is so much said in the Word of God about God's regarding the humble. Proud modern man doesn't seem to be an expert at displaying humility. In James 4:6 we read, "But he giveth more grace. Wherefore he saith, God resisteth the proud, but giveth grace unto the humble." We are told, "Humble yourselves therefore under the mighty hand of God, that he may exalt you in due time" (1 Pet. 5:6). There is a great deal said about humility in Scripture. It is something God takes note of and recognizes. David took a humble place. We read his words in Psalm 131:1, "LORD, my heart is not haughty, nor mine eyes lofty: neither do I exercise myself in great matters, or in things too high for me." In Isaiah 57:15 we are told, "For thus saith the high and lofty One that inhabiteth eternity, whose name is Holy; I dwell in the high and holy place, with him also that is of a contrite and humble spirit, to revive the spirit of the humble, and to revive the heart of the contrite ones." In 1 Peter 5:5 we read, "Likewise, ye younger, submit yourselves unto the elder. Yea, all of you be subject one to another, and be clothed with humility: for God resisteth the proud, and giveth grace to the humble." 1 Peter 3:4 tells us, "But let it be the hidden man of the heart, in that which is not corruptible, even the ornament of a meek and quiet spirit, which is in the sight of God of great price." All of these verses reveal how God regards humility.

> The LORD will perfect that which concerneth me: thy mercy, O LORD, endureth for ever: forsake not the works of thine own hands [Ps. 138:8].

This is the Old Testament way of saying, "Being confident of this very thing, that he which hath begun a good work in you will perform it until the day of Jesus Christ" (Phil. 1:6).

PSALM 139

THEME: A song of praise to the attributes of God

This psalm is "To the chief Musician, A Psalm of David." This is a theological psalm in that it reveals something of the attributes of God in relation to His creation. It reveals His omniscience, His omnipresence, and His omnipotence. These are what I call four-cylinder words, but they simply mean that God is all-knowing (omniscient), He is everywhere present (omnipresent), and He is all-powerful (omnipotent). God can do anything that is the object of His power. Sometimes the ridiculous question is asked, "Can God make a rock so big that He cannot lift it?" The answer to that is that God never does anything ridiculous.

This is a psalm that will answer several pertinent questions for us.

THE OMNISCIENCE OF GOD

O Lord, thou hast searched me, and known me [Ps. 139:1].

This speaks of the omniscience of God. He knows you. He knows me. He is the greatest psychologist. When you have a problem, it is not necessary to climb upon the psychiatrist's couch and tell him everything. Why don't you climb upon the couch of the Lord Jesus and just tell Him everything? You might as well tell Him because He knows all about you anyway. The psychiatrist still won't know you even after you have told him everything you can think of.

> **Thou knowest my downsitting and mine uprising, thou understandest my thought afar off.**
>
> **Thou compassest my path and my lying down, and art acquainted with all my ways.**

For there is not a word in my tongue, but lo, O LORD, thou knowest it altogether [Ps. 139:2–4].

That word that was on your tongue—perhaps you wanted to rip out a good strong oath, but you didn't do it because of the presence of someone. God saw it on your tongue. He knows everything. "There is not a word in my tongue, but, lo, O LORD, thou knowest it altogether."

Thou hast beset me behind and before, and laid thine hand upon me.

Such knowledge is too wonderful for me; it is high, I cannot attain unto it [Ps. 139:5–6].

You may ask, How can God do that? I don't know, and the psalmist says he doesn't know. "Such knowledge is too wonderful for me; it is high, I cannot attain unto it." Actually the omniscience of God is not an occasion for terror but for comfort. He saved me and yet He knew me—that is the amazing thing about it. There are some people whom you accept and receive, and then in some way they disappoint you. You thought you knew them, but you really did not know them. God knows us and yet He will save us. How wonderful He is! God knew David, and David let Him down. But God knew something about David's faith that we could not see. He could see David's heart, and beneath the faith that failed was a faith that never failed. The Lord knew what Simon Peter was going to do. He even knew that Judas would betray Him. Even though we don't understand it, that is the omniscience of God. He knows everything.

THE OMNIPRESENCE OF GOD

Let's look at the omnipresence of God for a moment. No matter where you go, you cannot get away from God.

Whither shall I go from thy spirit? or whither shall I flee from thy presence?

> **If I ascend up into heaven, thou art there: if I make my
> bed in hell, behold, thou art there [Ps. 139:7–8].**

"Hell" is Sheol (not hell), the region of the unseen and unknown. God
is there. No matter where you go, He is there.

> **If I take the wings of the morning, and dwell in the ut-
> termost parts of the sea [Ps. 139:9].**

You won't get away from God even if you go to the moon. To me it was
thrilling to hear those first three astronauts who went around the
moon and read the first chapter of Genesis on Christmas Eve. You
don't run away from God, my friend, even if you go to the moon!

> **Even there shall thy hand lead me, and thy right hand
> shall hold me.**
>
> **If I say, Surely the darkness shall cover me; even the
> night shall be light about me.**
>
> **Yea, the darkness hideth not from thee: but the night
> shineth as the day: the darkness and the light are both
> alike to thee [Ps. 139:10–12].**

A man once said to me, "Do you think we ought to confess our sins in
detail to God?" I said, "Of course. Spell them out. He already knows
about them anyway. He was present when you committed them; so you
better agree with Him on the subject. Let Him know that you recognize
it as sin." My friend, to confess your sin is to *agree* with God—God
says it is sin and you agree with Him that it is sin.

> **For thou hast possessed my reins: thou hast covered me
> in my mother's womb [Ps. 139:13].**

From the time we are conceived in the womb we never get away from
the presence of God in this life.

He reinforces this truth in the next verse:

> **I will praise thee; for I am fearfully and wonderfully made: marvellous are thy works; and that my soul knoweth right well [Ps. 139:14].**

God is everywhere, and man is a fabulous creature who has the attention of God constantly.

> **My substance was not hid from thee, when I was made in secret, and curiously wrought in the lowest parts of the earth.**
>
> **Thine eyes did see my substance, yet being unperfect; and in thy book all my members were written, which in continuance were fashioned, when as yet there was none of them [Ps. 139:15–16].**

Before the body was formed David says he was a person. He was a person as he was being formed in the womb. Even before the members of his body were formed, he was a person. The personhood is declared to take place at the very moment of conception.

This is very important in our day because of the question of abortion. I heard a minister of the liberal persuasion say that the Bible has nothing to say about abortion, and therefore we can make our own decision or do as we please. However, the Bible does have something to say about it, and here is a clear-cut reference. While the body was being formed, David said he was a person, a human being. God had the blueprint of his members before they came into existence. The person was there.

Now hear it straight: abortion is murder unless it is performed to save the mother's life or even the child's life. Abortion to get rid of the little unformed fellow before he has an opportunity to utter a cry in order to cover up sin or escape responsibility merely enhances the awful and cruel crime. Do not blame me for this charge. Blame David— he wrote it. Blame the Holy Spirit—He declared it.

The Bible has the answer to all the problems of life if we consider

all of it, and it does not always give the popular interpretation. It is
well to get God's viewpoint.

THE OMNIPOTENCE OF GOD

How precious also are thy thoughts unto me, O God!
how great is the sum of them!

If I should count them, they are more in number than
the sand: when I awake, I am still with thee [Ps.
139:17–18].

My friend, God *loves* us! And the God who loves us is omnipotent—
all-powerful!

Surely thou wilt slay the wicked, O God: depart from
me therefore, ye bloody men [Ps. 139:19].

We have both the wicked and the godly mentioned in this psalm. God
says that He will judge the wicked, and He will hear the prayer of His
people. Praise God that He is all-knowing, all-powerful, and present
everywhere.

PSALM 140

THEME: A prayer for deliverance from evil men

As we have gone through the Book of Psalms, we have come to groups of psalms that have been like a cluster of grapes, or a stalk of bananas, in that they were all related to the same bunch. Psalm 140 has no visible connection with the marvelous theological one hundred thirty-ninth psalm that preceded it. Psalm 140 sets before us in prophecy the last days when the godly remnant of Israel will face the Antichrist—that false messiah, the Man of Sin. It is a prayer of David, asking and praying for protection because evil men are about him. David was under some kind of pressure at this time, and we believe it was from the madman King Saul, who was the adumbration of the man of violence about whom the apostle Paul wrote in the second chapter of 2 Thessalonians.

This psalm has an application for you and me today. Many of us could pray this prayer.

> **Deliver me, O Lord, from the evil man; preserve me from the violent man [Ps. 140:1].**

In this verse is a designation of the Antichrist. He is called the "evil man" and the "violent man." But John says there are many antichrists. "Little children, it is the last time: and as ye have heard that antichrist shall come, even now are there many antichrists; whereby we know that it is the last time" (1 John 2:18). I am sure that many of us have come in contact with evil men. David's prayer is that he might be preserved and delivered from these evil men. That has always been my prayer in the ministry: "Oh, God, do not let me fall under the influence or the power of an evil man." It is also dangerous for a minister to be under the influence or power of any one man or under the power of a little clique in a church. It is not only dangerous; it is dynamite.

> Which imagine mischiefs in their heart; continually are
> they gathered together for war.

> They have sharpened their tongues like a serpent; ad-
> ders' poison is under their lips. Selah [Ps. 140:2–3].

Paul speaks of the human race in the same manner (Rom. 3:10–18).
Human beings have tongues filled with poison. The tongue can destroy as much as any atom bomb. It can ruin a man's reputation and
blacken his life.

> Keep me, O Lord, from the hands of the wicked; pre-
> serve me from the violent man; who have purposed to
> overthrow my goings [Ps. 140:4].

This is David's prayer, and it is also a prayer that the remnant will pray
during the Great Tribulation. This is not a prayer for Christians in this
day of grace. However, for the people who are in the Great Tribulation
Period and back under law, I see no reason why they shouldn't pray
this prayer for divine judgment and for divine wrath.

> Grant not, O Lord, the desires of the wicked: further not
> his wicked device; lest they exalt themselves. Selah.

> As for the head of those that compass me about, let the
> mischief of their own lips cover them.

> Let burning coals fall upon them: let them be cast into
> the fire; into deep pits, that they rise not up again [Ps.
> 140:8–10].

The psalmist is praying against that wicked man, the Antichrist. As I
have said before, this is not the kind of prayer a believer should pray.
Rather, we should follow the instruction in Romans 12:19–21, "Dearly
beloved, avenge not yourselves, but rather give place unto wrath: for it
is written, Vengeance is mine; I will repay, saith the Lord. Therefore if
thine enemy hunger, feed him; if he thirst, give him drink: for in so

doing thou shalt heap coals of fire on his head. Bo not overcome of evll, but overcome evil with good." In other words, don't let yourself become bitter. Don't get carried away with enmity and revenge, which will separate you from a walk of faith. God will take care of things. It has been my experience that when we keep our hands off, God will generally move in and deal with those who attempt to thwart and hinder God's work. Vengeance belongs to God. Turn the case over to Him. Then you can do something good for the individual who has injured you. God puts us in an unusual place.

> **Let not an evil speaker be established in the earth: evil shall hunt the violent man to overthrow him [Ps. 140:11].**

There is sure victory if we do not forsake the path of faith. "For whatsoever is born of God overcometh the world: and this is the victory that overcometh the world, even our faith" (1 John 5:4). The wicked tongue is not going to be established or survive. The lie will finally be made known. Satan was a liar from the beginning, and he has a lot of his urchins running around today following his example. Someday they will all be exposed as liars.

PSALM 141

THEME: A prayer to be delivered from evil

This psalm was written by David. It has something to do with his personal history. He sends out an SOS. His prayer arises from some unknown experience but probably comes from the time that he was fleeing from Saul. The application is to the remnant of Israel in the final struggle against evil, but it also has a message for us today.

> LORD, I cry unto thee: make haste unto me; give ear unto my voice, when I cry unto thee.
>
> Let my prayer be set forth before thee as incense; and the lifting up of my hands as the evening sacrifice [Ps. 141:1–2].

One commentator has said, "David was in love with prayer." He was a great man of prayer. He mentions the fact that prayer is like sweet incense. Today, when we pray and praise in the name of Christ, that prayer is like the sweet incense that went up out of the tabernacle when Aaron, the high priest, sprinkled incense on the golden altar. "Let my prayer be set forth before thee as incense."

However, to be sweet incense, that prayer would have to be backed up by an obedient life. The Lord Jesus made it abundantly clear that if we expect God to hear and answer our prayers, we must live lives that are obedient to Him. The idea that we can live any way we want to and expect God to answer our prayer is a big mistake. The Lord said, "If ye shall ask any thing in my name, I will do it." But He did not stop there. He continued, "If ye love me, keep my commandments" (John 14:14–15). If you expect Him to answer your prayers, you must be obedient. We need to pray in the name of Christ, yes, but also we need a life to back it up.

Set a watch, O Lord, before my mouth; keep the door of my lips [Ps. 141:3].

David says, "Oh, Lord, don't let my lips and my life contradict each other." He learned this lesson by bitter experience. And we need to pray, "Don't let me pray one thing on Sunday and live something else on Monday."

Incline not my heart to any evil thing, to practise wicked works with men that work iniquity: and let me not eat of their dainties.

Let the righteous smite me; it shall be a kindness: and let him reprove me; it shall be an excellent oil, which shall not break my head: for yet my prayer also shall be in their calamities [Ps. 141:4–5].

There are many men who work and make their living in this evil world. There is no question that they rub up against evil every day; and, as the saying goes, the boat should be in the ocean, but it is tragic when the ocean is in the boat. When a man lives in the world, and acts like the world, and lives like the Devil's child all week, he cannot expect the Heavenly Father to answer his prayer on Sunday. Psalm 66:18 says, "If I regard iniquity in my heart, the Lord will not hear me." God has not promised to hear the prayer of the wicked. Instead we are told that ". . . the effectual fervent prayer of a righteous man availeth much" (James 5:16). First John 3:22 says, "And whatsoever we ask, we receive of him, because we keep his *commandments*, and *do* those things that are pleasing in his sight." David wanted the Lord to keep the door of his lips. He did not want to incline his heart toward any evil thing. We must follow his example if we want our prayers to be powerful before Almighty God.

But mine eyes are unto thee, O God the Lord: in thee is my trust; leave not my soul destitute.

Keep me from the snares which they have laid for me,
and the gins of the workers of iniquity [Ps. 141:8–9].

David prays that he will not fall into the trap of the wicked. The Devil attempts to trip us up all the time, and he uses all kinds of devices. Unfortunately, we are not aware of many of his traps. We are not even as wise as the carnal Christians in Corinth to whom Paul said, ". . . we are not ignorant of his devices" (2 Cor. 2:11). Some of us seem to be woefully ignorant of Satan's devices. Oh, my friend, let us pray to be delivered from evil so that our prayers may be potent prayers.

PSALM 142

THEME: The beginning of David's suffering

Notice that this is a maschil psalm, that is, a psalm of instruction. It is a psalm from which you and I can learn something. This, again, is a great prayer of David. Where was he when he prayed this prayer? The inspired text gives this inscription: "Maschil of David; A Prayer when he was in the cave."

> **I cried unto the LORD with my voice; with my voice unto the LORD did I make my supplication [Ps. 142:1].**

We are not told which cave he was hiding in at this time. The cave of En-gedi is mentioned in 1 Samuel 24. I passed by En-gedi when I was in that land. They have made a new road down by the Dead Sea which goes all the way from Jericho up to Masada. It is very interesting country. The road has opened up that area to tourists. When I saw En-gedi I realized that it would be a very good place in which to hide.

Also there is the cave of Adullam, which is the cave where David went to hide the first time he left Israel to escape from King Saul. Both of these caves are known. My guess is that he was in Adullam when he wrote this psalm. We know that it was at this time that " . . every one that was in distress, and every one that was in debt, and every one that was discontented, gathered themselves unto him . . ." (1 Sam. 22:2). About four hundred men came to him at this time.

Now notice his prayer at this time:

> **I poured out my complaint before him; I shewed before him my trouble [Ps. 142:2].**

In other words, David laid out before God everything that was in his heart and life. That is the way you and I should pray. This idea that we should "pray around" something, or rationalize in our prayers, or pray "all around Robin Hood's barn," is wrong. We ought to get right down to the nitty-gritty and tell God everything in our lives. David said, "I shewed before him my trouble." My friend, you can tell Him about your temptations; you can tell Him about everything.

Years ago Fenelon wrote a wonderful thing along this line, which he has entitled "Tell God":

Tell God all that is in your heart, as one unloads one's heart, its pleasures and its pains, to a dear friend. Tell Him your troubles, that He may comfort you; tell Him your joys, that He may sober them; tell Him your longings, that He may purify them; tell Him your dislikes, that He may help you to conquer them; talk to Him of your temptations, that He may shield you from them; show Him the wounds of your heart, that He may heal them; lay bare your indifference to good, your depraved tastes for evil, your instability. Tell Him how self-love makes you unjust to others, how vanity tempts you to be insincere, how pride disguises you to yourself as to others.

If you thus pour out all your weaknesses, needs, troubles, there will be no lack of what to say. You will never exhaust the subject. It is continually being renewed. People who have no secrets from each other never want subjects of conversation. They do not weigh their words, for there is nothing to be held back; neither do they seek for something to say. They talk out of the abundance of the heart, without consideration, just what they think. Blessed are they who attain to such familiar, unreserved intercourse with God.

My friend, David had that marvelous relationship with Almighty God, and he told God all that was in his heart.

Notice that David said, "I poured out my complaint before him; I shewed before him my trouble." David, as a young man, was anointed king of Israel. In the court of King Saul, that mad king threw a javelin at David, trying to pin David to the wall, but he missed, and David had to flee for his life. He complained that he was hunted like a partridge.

It was open season on him all of the time, and he had to keep running. Out of that situation this young man lifts his heart and cries out to God.

> **When my spirit was overwhelmed within me, then thou knewest my path. In the way wherein I walked have they privily [secretly] laid a snare for me [Ps. 142:3].**

They tried to trap David. David looked to the Lord for help, and God guided him.

> **I looked on my right hand, and beheld, but there was no man that would know me: refuge failed me; no man cared for my soul [Ps. 142:4].**

This was David's situation when he first left the court of Saul, but afterward, as we have seen, four hundred men joined him. He knew God was responsible for this support.

> **I cried unto thee, O LORD: I said, Thou art my refuge and my portion in the land of the living [Ps. 142:5].**

There are two things we ought to note. He hid in the cave—if he had not hidden, Saul would have killed him. But, you may say, he was trusting the Lord. Yes, he was trusting the Lord, but the Lord expected him to use good old sanctified common sense.

PSALM 143

This is another marvelous prayer of David. It is an urgent appeal for help. David had no inhibitions, and he opened his heart to God. Oh, that we could learn to pray like that!

> **Hear my prayer, O LORD, give ear to my supplications: in thy faithfulness answer me, and in thy righteousness [Ps. 143:1].**

David appeals to the faithfulness and righteousness of God for an answer. Isn't this exactly what believers are to do when they sin? "If we confess our sins, he is faithful and just to forgive us our sins, and to cleanse us from all unrighteousness" (1 John 1:9). "He is faithful and just [or righteous]." Like David, we appeal to God on the basis of His faithfulness and His righteousness. This psalm is a very wonderful prayer, and it can fit into your experience and mine.

This is also the plea of the nation Israel. This is their hope when they cry for help from God in their day of calamity. And God will not disappoint them.

God is not through with Israel. In Micah 7:20 we read, "Thou wilt perform the truth to Jacob, and the mercy to Abraham, which thou hast sworn unto our fathers from the days of old." In Exodus 2:24–25 we are told, "And God heard their groaning, and God remembered his covenant with Abraham, with Isaac, and with Jacob. And God looked upon the children of Israel, and God had respect unto them." Why did God have respect unto Israel? Because he is faithful and righteous.

In Romans Paul tells us what Israel's problem is today. "For they being ignorant of God's righteousness, and going about to establish their own righteousness, have not submitted themselves unto the righteousness of God" (Rom. 10:3). This is also the trouble the Gentiles have. They are working at a religion. They are trying to do something to please God. My friend, He has already *done* something for them. He sent His Son to the cross to pay the penalty for sin. You please Him when you accept what He has done for you. "For Christ is the end of the law for righteousness to every one that believeth" (Rom. 10:4).

> **I stretch forth my hands unto thee: my soul thirsteth after thee, as a thirsty land. Selah [Ps. 143:6].**

I have watched it rain out on the desert on that sandy soil when it has rained and rained and *rained,* and that thirsty land just drinks it up. David says, "My soul thirsteth after thee, as a thirsty land."

Now hear David's cry:

> **Hear me speedily, O Lord: my spirit faileth: hide not thy face from me, lest I be like unto them that go down into the pit [Ps. 143:7].**

David is saying to God, "You are my only help."

> **Cause me to hear thy lovingkindness in the morning; for in thee do I trust: cause me to know the way wherein I should walk; for I lift up my soul unto thee.**
>
> **Deliver me, O Lord, from mine enemies: I flee unto thee to hide me.**
>
> **Teach me to do thy will; for thou art my God: thy spirit is good; lead me into the land of uprightness [Ps. 143:8–10].**

This reveals David's trust in God as his only refuge and his only hope.

"Teach me to do thy will; for thou art my God" should be the daily prayer of every child of God.

PSALM 144

THEME: Praise and prayer to God because of who He is

This is another one of the psalms written by David. Some of the contents are similar to those in Psalm 18, which began, "I will love thee, O LORD, my strength. The LORD is my rock, and my fortress, and my deliverer; my God, my strength, in whom I will trust; my buckler, and the horn of my salvation, and my high tower" (Ps. 18:1–2). Further down in the psalm David said, "In my distress I called upon the LORD, and cried unto my God: he heard my voice out of his temple, and my cry came before him, even into his ears" (Ps. 18:6). This psalm was written out of one of David's experiences when he was delivered out of the hand of King Saul. Also it is prophetic, looking forward to that coming day when the children of Israel will suffer during the Great Tribulation. In this time of great distress they will turn to God in prayer. Also this psalm is applicable to all the saints during the centuries between David's time and the Great Tribulation period.

Blessed be the LORD my strength, which teacheth my hands to war, and my fingers to fight [Ps. 144:1].

What does David mean? There will be those who will immediately jump at this and say, "Look, the God of the Old Testament is warlike." My friend, if you had lived in David's day, you would have been a lot more comfortable knowing that you were protected from the enemy surrounding you and knowing that you *could* defend yourself.

It is entirely incorrect to say that the Lord Jesus Christ was a pacifist. He gives peace to the human heart, and peace with God through the forgiveness of sins; but He also said, ". . . a strong man armed keepeth his [house] palace . . ." (Luke 11:21), which is what David is saying in this psalm. It is true that our Lord is the Prince of Peace, but He has made it very clear that there will be no peace on this earth until He returns. In the meantime it is more comfortable to know that our nation has enough armaments to protect us. I only hope we don't get some fanatic in power who will get rid of our protection, maintaining that we can depend on the goodness of human nature to take care of us. That type of thinking brought many a nation down into the dust. Some of the Greek states tried it. They had an outstanding civilization, but they are in ruin and rubble today because they could not protect themselves.

> **My goodness, and my fortress; my high tower, and my deliverer; my shield, and he in whom I trust; who subdueth my people under me [Ps. 144:2].**

David says that God is his goodness. If you and I have any righteousness, it is Christ. David says that God is also his Goodness, his Protector, his Fortress, his High Tower, his Deliverer, and his Shield. Although it is comforting to know that our nation has an arsenal to protect us, I also want to make sure that God is my protector, that He is my fortress, my high tower, my deliverer, and my shield.

"Who subdueth my people under me" is David speaking as a commander.

> **LORD, what is man, that thou takest knowledge of him! or the son of man, that thou makest account of him! [Ps. 144:3].**

Why should God take note of little man? Frankly, man does not amount to very much.

> **Man is like to vanity: his days are as a shadow that passeth away [Ps. 144:4].**

"Man is like to vanity" means that man is nothing without God, that life is purposeless without Him.

When I was a pastor in Nashville, a man walked into my study one day holding a rusty old gun—it looked like a .45 to me. He said, "If you can't give me a reason to live, I am going to kill myself." I replied,

"Well, you sure are putting me on the spot; I can't think of any reason why you shouldn't kill yourself, but I do want to tell you that you are not going to solve your problem by taking your life. All you will be doing is removing your problem from earth and taking it to a place where there is no solution, because you will fix your eternal destiny. But here and now you can make a decision for God which will add purpose to your life, and you won't be in such a hurry to end it. Then, when you do die, you will go home to be with Christ, your Savior."

Life without God is quite empty. I have a newspaper clipping which tells about a Swedish man who inherited what is said to be the largest fortune in the world, $5 billion—that is a lot of money! But that man took his own life. His $5 billion dollars didn't keep him here. He found life rather purposeless. My friend, without Jesus Christ, without God, "man is like to vanity" and emptiness. Without God life has no purpose.

Now listen to David plead with God.

Bow thy heavens, O LORD, and come down: touch the mountains, and they shall smoke [Ps. 144:5].

This is a call for God to break into human events, for God to intrude into human history. This is confirmed in Isaiah 64:1–2 which says, "Oh that thou wouldest rend the heavens, that thou wouldest come down, that the mountains might flow down at thy presence, As when the melting fire burneth, the fire causeth the waters to boil, to make thy name known to thine adversaries, that the nations may tremble at thy presence!" God is going to intrude into human history one day. I don't want to take a fanatical position and say that He is going to do it tomorrow, or even in this century, but the fact is that He is going to do it.

Cast forth lightning, and scatter them: shoot out thine arrows, and destroy them [Ps. 144:6].

When the Lord comes again, He is coming in judgment. The whole tenor of Scripture, including the New Testament, is that the Lord is coming in judgment one day. There is no more vivid and dramatic picture of this than the one given in Revelation 19:11, where John saw heaven opened and beheld a white horse, ". . . and he that sat upon him was called Faithful and True, and in righteousness he doth judge and make war." That is a picture of the Lord Jesus Christ coming forth as a conqueror to conquer. Maybe you don't like this picture, but it is the picture that the Word of God presents.

At that time, the psalmist says:

> **I will sing a new song unto thee, O God: upon a psaltery and an instrument of ten strings will I sing praises unto thee [Ps. 144:9].**

Not until after the Tribulation will the children of Israel be able to sing this new song unto their God.

PSALM 145

THEME: Praise for what God is and for what He does

This is the last psalm that mentions David as the author. He may have written some of the psalms that do not name an author, but we cannot be sure. This psalm is an acrostic, which means that each verse begins with one of the letters of the Hebrew alphabet.

Immediately we run into a problem which the critics have latched onto—there are twenty-two Hebrew letters and only twenty-one verses in this psalm. The psalm begins with *Aleph*, the first letter of the alphabet, and ends with *Tau*, the final letter in the Hebrew alphabet; the missing letter is *Nun*. Some critics say that *Nun* was left out by some transcriber. I don't think that is the case at all. I believe it was left out for a very definite reason. From Psalm 145 to 150 we find that every one of them is a hallelujah psalm. It is an increasing crescendo. Why would one verse be left out of Psalm 145? I think it speaks of the fact that our praise is imperfect. I like what F.W. Grant has written relative to the omission of this one letter: "I cannot but conclude that the gap is meant to remind us that in fact the fullness of praise is not complete without other voices, which are not found here, and that these missing voices are those of the Church and the heavenly saints in general." You don't get all of the hallelujahs until you get to the nineteenth chapter of Revelation: "And after these things I heard a great voice of much people in heaven, saying, Alleluia; Salvation, and glory, and honour, and power, unto the Lord our God . . . . And again they said, Alleluia. And her smoke rose up for ever and ever . . . . And I heard as it were the voice of a great multitude, and as the voice of many waters, and as the voice of mighty thunderings, saying, Alleluia: for the Lord God omnipotent reigneth (Rev. 19:1, 3, 6). There is the missing hallelujah. The praise in this Psalm 145 is not quite complete—nor is it in any of the psalms. At the occasion of the birth of Jesus, the angels said, "Glory to God in the highest . . ." (Luke 2:14). Why? Because Jesus was born in Bethlehem and there would be peace. But there hasn't been peace. We have never been able to sing the Hallelujah chorus perfectly yet. But there is coming a day when Christ will return to this earth. The day that He comes forth will be a great day, and then the Hallelujah chorus will be sung correctly and completely.

> **I will extol thee, my God, O king; and I will bless thy name for ever and ever.**
>
> **Every day will I bless thee; and I will praise thy name for ever and ever [Ps. 145:1–2].**

"Every day will I bless thee"—this is not for only one day in the week when we go to church but for every day. There are days when we don't feel like blessing Him. We sometimes sing, "We praise Him for all that is past, and trust Him for all that is to come." We can change that around and sing, "We trust Him for all that is past and praise Him for all that is to come."

This is a marvelous psalm of praise!

> **The LORD is gracious, and full of compassion; slow to anger, and of great mercy [Ps. 145:8].**

We have a kind God. David had experienced the kindness of God, and it motivated him to show the same kindness of God to others.

> **The LORD is righteous in all his ways, and holy in all his works.**
>
> **The LORD is nigh unto all them that call upon him, to all that call upon him in truth [Ps. 145:17–18].**

Whoever you are and wherever you are, if you mean business with God, you can come into His presence through Christ. "The LORD is nigh [He is near] unto all them that call upon him." There are many folk who are stiff-arming God. That is one reason they go through a church ritual—they are escaping a personal confrontation with Him.

One of the great doctrines that the Reformation brought back to us was the doctrine of the "priesthood of believers." If you have trusted Jesus Christ as your Savior, you have direct *access* to God. If you are unsaved, God invites you to come to Him for salvation. God is available.

PSALM 146

THEME: A Hallelujah psalm, praise to God for His goodness

The five psalms that conclude this great hymn book are all hallelujah psalms. Notice that they begin with "Praise ye the LORD" and end with "Praise ye the LORD," which means, of course, "hallelujah." No longer do they tell anything of persecution or suffering; there are no prayers for help or deliverance from the enemy; there are no imprecatory prayers. The night of sin and suffering is over. Weeping is past and joy has come in the morning of the Millennium (See Ps. 30:5).

> **Praise ye the LORD. Praise the LORD, O my soul [Ps. 146:1].**

Not only should we praise God with our lips, but we should genuinely praise Him from the heart.

> **Put not your trust in princes, nor in the son of man, in whom there is no help [Ps. 146:3].**

This verse describes the powerlessness of man. No lasting help can come from any human being whose body will one day return to the dust from which it was made, whether he be a prince or a common man.

Dr. A.C. Gaebelein told of a visit he had from an orthodox Jew. I'll let him tell it in his own words: "He stated that he had read the New Testament and found the title of Jesus of Nazareth so often mentioned as 'the son of man.' He then declared that there is a warning in the Old Testament not to trust the son of man. As we asked him for the passage he quoted from this Psalm, 'Trust not . . . in the son of man in whom is no salvation.' We explained to him that if our Lord had been only the son of man and nothing else, if He had not been Immanuel, the virgin-born Son of God, if it were not true as Isaiah stated it, that He is the child born and *the Son* given, there would be no salvation in Him. But He came God's Son and appeared in the form of man for our redemption. His argument showed the blindness of the Jew. The statement is given in this psalm, that man is sinful, that there is no hope in man, he is a finite creature and turns to dust. There is but One in whom salvation and all man's needs is found, the God of Jacob, the loving Jehovah" (*The Book of Psalms*, p. 500–501).

In the closing verses of this psalm, "the LORD," meaning *Jehovah*, is mentioned eight times.

> Happy is he that hath the God of Jacob for his help, whose hope is in the LORD his God:
>
> Which made heaven, and earth, the sea, and all that therein is: which keepeth truth for ever:
>
> Which executed judgment for the oppressed: which giveth food to the hungry. The LORD looseth the prisoners:
>
> The LORD openeth the eyes of the blind: the LORD raiseth them that are bowed down: the LORD loveth the righteous [Ps. 146:5–8].

God is the One who is in the *helping* business.

> The LORD preserveth the strangers; he relieveth the fatherless and widow: but the way of the wicked he turneth upside down.
>
> The LORD shall reign for ever, even thy God, O Zion, unto all generations. Praise ye the LORD [Ps. 146:9–10].

As Jehovah, He is Redeemer. As Creator, He is Elohim. The Psalms make this abundantly clear. "Praise ye the LORD"—Hallelujah!

PSALM 147

THEME: A hallelujah chorus because of God's goodness to the earth and to Jerusalem

Praise ye the LORD: for it is good to sing praises unto our God; for it is pleasant; and praise is comely.

The LORD doth build up Jerusalem: he gathereth together the outcasts of Israel. [Ps. 147:1–2].

As you can see, this has not yet been accomplished, but has a future fulfillment.

He healeth the broken in heart, and bindeth up their wounds [Ps. 147:3].

God will do this for those who have passed through the horrors of the Great Tribulation. And, friend, He does it for you and me.

He telleth the number of the stars; he calleth them all by their names [Ps. 147:4].

What a contrast! He who cares for our broken hearts is the same God who not only knows the number of the stars—a number so vast that no human figures can express it—but has a name for each one!

Praise the LORD, O Jerusalem; praise thy God, O Zion.

For he hath strengthened the bars of thy gates; he hath blessed thy children within thee.

He maketh peace in thy borders, and filleth thee with the finest of the wheat [Ps. 147:12–14].

The King has come to Jerusalem, the Lord Jesus Christ, the King of Peace. At this time the prediction of Isaiah will be fulfilled, "O thou afflicted, tossed with tempest, and not comforted, behold, I will lay thy stones with fair colours, and lay thy foundations with sapphires. And I will make thy windows of agates, and thy gates of carbuncles, and all thy borders of pleasant stones. And all thy children shall be taught of the LORD: and great shall be the peace of thy children" (Isa. 54:11–13).

> **He hath not dealt so with any nation: and as for his judgments, they have not known them. Praise ye the LORD [Ps. 147:20].**

The nation of Israel is unique. They are the *only* people given the title "Chosen People." They are the only ones made custodians of the revelation of God. In His Word God says he has an eternal purpose for them.

We are to pray for the peace of Jerusalem, for the time that God will fulfill His promise to them.

PSALM 148

THEME: *A hallelujah chorus of all God's created intelligences*

In this psalm praise begins with the heavenlies. What a great hallelujah chorus this will be when all God's created intelligences in heaven and in earth will praise Him!

> **Praise ye the LORD. Praise ye the LORD from the heavens: praise him in the heights.**
>
> **Praise ye him, all his angels: praise ye him, all his hosts.**
>
> **Praise ye him, sun and moon: praise him, all ye stars of light [Ps. 148:1–3].**

The praise starts in the highest heaven, the third heaven, where it includes believers, I think.

> **Kings of the earth, and all people; princes, and all judges of the earth:**
>
> **Both young men, and maidens; old men, and children:**
>
> **Let them praise the name of the LORD: for his name alone is excellent; his glory is above the earth and heaven [Ps. 148:11–13].**

Not only in the heavenlies, but on the earth as well, will His created beings praise Him. This is moving now to a mighty crescendo when heaven and earth will praise God!

PSALM 149

THEME: *A hallelujah chorus because the kingdom has come through redemption by blood, and judgment by power*

Praise ye the LORD. Sing unto the LORD a now song, and his praise in tho congregation of saints [Ps. 149:1].

We have already discussed the "new song" that is spoken of in the Book of Revelation. The new song will be about the fact that the Lord Jesus is our Redeemer.

Let Israel rejoice in him that made him: let the children of Zion be joyful in their King [Ps. 149:1].

He is our Redeemer and let us remember that He is our Creator. We should praise Him for that. When we climb to a mountaintop or walk down by the ocean, we can praise Him. When we are flying by plane, it is a good time to praise the Lord.

Now notice that we have here the judgment of the nations.

Let the high praises of God be in their mouth, and a two-edged sword in their hand;

To execute vengeance upon the heathen, and punishments upon the people;

To bind their kings with chains, and their nobles with fetters of iron;

To execute upon them the judgment written: this honour have all his saints. Praise ye the LORD [Ps. 149:6–9].

Let's keep in mind that when the Lord Jesus returns to this earth, He will not be welcomed by the nations of the world. He is coming to judge this earth. When He returns to this little planet, He will put down the rebellion that has broken out; and He will break them with the rod of iron. As it is said in Psalm 2, "Thou shalt break them with a rod of iron; thou shalt dash them in pieces like a potter's vessel" (Ps. 2:9). Oh, my friend, let's not be deluded by this namby-pamby way of thinking that our God is not going to judge. You and I are living in a world that is moving to a judgment day.

PSALM 150

THEME: The grand finale of the hallelujah chorus, with choir and orchestra

Praise ye the Lord. Praise God in his sanctuary: praise him in the firmament of his power.

Praise him for his mighty acts: praise him according to his excellent greatness.

Praise him with the sound of the trumpet: praise him with the psaltery and harp.

Praise him with the timbrel and dance: praise him with stringed instruments and organs.

Praise him upon the loud cymbals: praise him upon the high sounding cymbals.

Let every thing that hath breath praise the Lord. Praise ye the Lord [Ps. 150:1–6].

WHAT IS WORSHIP?

First of all we will consider the object of worship. This will require that we answer, in a general sort of way, the question: What is worship? To do this we shall deal with one statement found in Psalm 150:1; "Praise ye the Lord." In this first aspect the emphasis is on "Praise ye the Lord." He is the object of worship.

The Psalms put the emphasis upon two things: the fact that He is the Creator, and the fact that He is the Redeemer. God made this earth on which we live, as well as the universe. This lovely sunshine that you are enjoying is His. He is the Creator. There is not a thing at your fingertips today that He did not make. He is worthy of our worship because He is the Creator. He is also worthy of our worship because He is the Redeemer. He is the *only* Creator, and He is the *only* Redeemer.

You see, God works in a field where He has no competition at all. He has a monopoly on the field of creation and on the field of redemption. Because of this, He claims from all of His creatures their worship, their adoration, and their praise.

And the Scriptures say that God is a jealous God. I can't find where He asks me to apologize for Him for this. He has created us for Himself. He has redeemed us for Himself. On the human level, marriage is used to illustrate the believer's relationship to Christ. A husband, if he loves his wife, does not share her with other men. He is jealous of her. Her love is to be for him alone. So believers, called in the Scripture the bride of Christ, are created solely for Him. He alone is to have our adoration; He alone is to have our praise. You will recall that John, on the Isle of Patmos, felt constrained to fall down and worship the angel who had been so helpful in bringing all of the visions before him, but the angel rebuked him and said, ". . . See thou do it not . . . worship God" (Rev. 22:9). He does not want even His angels worshiped; He does not want Mary worshiped; He wants none worshiped but Himself. He alone is *worthy* of worship. And Scriptures say there is coming a day when everything that has breath will praise the Lord. He has created everything that it might praise Him.

WHO IS TO WORSHIP?

God is the *object* of worship, but this question follows: Who can worship?

The psalmist said: "Let every thing that hath breath praise the LORD. Praise ye the LORD" (Ps. 150:6). The emphasis now is upon ye. He is saying to mankind, "Praise ye the LORD." God apparently created man for the purposes of fellowship with Himself and that man might praise Him. There is no other reason for man's existence. What is the chief end of man? Man's chief end is to glorify God and enjoy Him forever.

God created the universe that it might glorify Him. It was not brought into existence for you and me. In the ages past—how far back we do not know—Job said: "When the morning stars sang together, and all the sons of God shouted for joy" (Job 38:7). They were praising

God. And the psalmist said: "For all the gods of the nations are idols: but the Lord made the heavens" (Ps. 96:5). He made the heavens that they might be a musical instrument to sing forth His praises throughout the eternal ages of the future. Although man was created for that high purpose, he got out of harmony, he got out of tune with God. He got out of fellowship with God. Perhaps Shakespeare expressed it when he gave to one of his characters in *The Merchant of Venice* these lines:

> There's not the smallest orb which thou behold'st
> But in his motion like an angel sings,
> Still quiring to the young-eyed cherubims;
> Such harmony is in immortal souls;
> But whilst this muddy vesture of decay
> Doth grossly close it in, we cannot hear it.
>
> (Act V, Scene 1)

Today you and I are living in a created universe that is actually singing praises to God. But man is out of tune. Man is in discord. God's great purpose is to bring man back into the harmony of heaven.

Let us move on now into the realm of music, about which I know nothing, but have made careful inquiry. I am reliably informed that on every good pipe organ there are four principal stops. There is the main stop known as Diapason; then there is the Flute stop; another which is known as the String stop; and then that which is known as Vox Humana (the human voice). I am told that the Vox Humana stop is very seldom in tune. If you put it in tune while the auditorium is cold, it would be out of tune when the auditorium is heated. And if you put it in tune when the auditorium is heated, it would be out of tune when the auditorium got cold. My beloved, it is hard to keep vox Humana in tune.

This great universe of God's is a mighty instrument. One day Jesus Christ went to the console of God's great organ, His creation, and He pulled out the stop known as Diapason. When He did this, the solar and stellar spaces broke into mighty song. Then He reached over and pulled out the Flute stop, and these little feathered friends, called birds, began to sing. Then when He reached out and pulled the String stop, light went humming across God's universe, and the angels lifted their voices in praise. Then He reached over and pulled out the Vox Humana—but it was out of tune. The great Organist was not only a musician, He knew how to repair the organ, so He left the console of the organ yonder in heaven, and He came down to this earth. Through redemption, the giving of His own, He was able to bring man back into harmony with God's tremendous creation. And, my beloved, today the redeemed are the ones to lift their voices in praise. Only the redeemed are in tune. The psalmist sings: "O give thanks unto the LORD, for he is good: for his mercy endureth for ever. Let the redeemed of the LORD say so, whom he hath redeemed from the hand of the enemy" (Ps. 107:1–2). And, brother, if the redeemed don't say so, no one will! Oh, to be in tune with heaven! Today sin has intruded into this world and has taken man out of God's choir; but individuals can come back in— and many have—through Jesus Christ, the son of David (David, the sweet singer of Israel). The Lord Jesus Christ has brought man back into a redemptive and right relationship with his Creator and Redeemer so that man can lift his voice in praise to Him.

WHY WORSHIP?

Now we want to answer the question: Why worship?

At this point we move our emphasis over from "Praise ye the LORD." We move the accent over to the verb, to that which is active. "*Praise* ye the Lord."

Very few people actually worship God. There really is no such thing as public worship. It was the great Chrysostom who put it like this: "The angels glorify; men scrutinize; Angels raise their voices in praise; men in disputation; They conceal their faces with their wings; but man with a presumptuous gaze would look into thine unspeakable glory." Oh, today, how many actually go to the church to worship? Somebody, in a very facetious manner, said that some people go to church to eye the clothes, and others to close their eyes. I wonder how many go to church for the purpose of worshiping God. Worship is divine intoxication. If you don't believe that, there is a fine illustration of it in the Book of Acts. On the Day of Pentecost Simon Peter got up and preached a sermon. We talk a great deal about that sermon, but actually it was an explanation to the people that these Spirit-filled men were not drunk. Drunkenness was not the explanation. How many would get the impression that *we* are intoxicated with God today? We need an ecclesiastical ecstasy. We need a theological thrill in this day in which we live.

There are three words that we must associate with worship, and these three words denote an experience of the human heart and the human soul as it comes into God's presence to worship.

The first of these words is *prostration*. In the Orient, people are accustomed to get down on their faces; in the West, we talk a great deal about having a dignified service. Now don't misunderstand me. I am not contending for a posture of the body. Victor Hugo once said that the soul is on its knees many times, regardless of the position of the body. I am not trying to insist on a posture of the body, but we do need to have our *souls* prostrated before God. The two prominent Bible words are the Hebrew *hishtahaweh*, meaning "to bow the neck," and the Greek *proskuneo*, meaning "to bow the knee" to God. And today we need to bow before God in heaven. The book of Revelation does not tell us much about heaven, but one thing we are sure about—every time we read of someone in heaven they are either getting down on their faces to worship God, or getting up off their faces from worshiping God. And, friend, if you don't like to worship God, you wouldn't like heaven because that is the thing with which they are occupied. Most of the time they are worshiping God, prostrating themselves down before Him. Beloved, we need that today.

When my spiritual life gets frayed and fuzzy at the edges and begins to tear at the seams, I like to get alone, get down on my face before Him, and pour out my heart to Him. Friend, when was the last time you got down on your face before God? When was the last time that you prostrated yourself before Him? Oh, it would do us good. It would take us out of the deep-freeze. It would deliver us from the shell in which we live. It would create within our hearts a different attitude if we would learn to prostrate our souls before God.

The second word that goes with worship is the word *adoration*. It is a term of endearment. There is passion in that word. "O worship the LORD in the beauty of holiness . . ." (Ps. 96:9). Worship is a love affair; it is making love to God. Michal, the first wife of David, resented his devotion to God. When King David brought the ark into Jerusalem, the record tells us: "So David and all the house of Israel brought up the ark of the LORD with shouting, and with the wound of the trumpet. And as the ark of the LORD came into the city of David, Michal Saul's daughter looked through a window, and saw king David leaping and dancing before the LORD; and she despised him in her heart" (2 Sam. 6:15–16). She despised him. Sure she did. She discovered that David loved God more than he loved her and that he was making love to God. Worship without love is like a flame without heat; it is like a rainbow without color; it is like a flower without perfume. Worship should have a spontaneity. It should not be synthetic. It should have an expectancy, a tenderness, and an eagerness in it. My friend, some types of worship compare to going downtown, sitting in a department store window, and holding the hand of a mannequin in there. It has no more life in it; it has no more vitality in it than that! Oh, to have a heart that goes out to God in adoration and in love to Him.

A young fellow wrote a love letter to his girl. He waxed eloquent and said: "I would climb the highest mountain for you. I would swim the widest river for you. I would crawl across burning sands of the desert for you." Then he put a P.S. at the end: "If it doesn't rain Wednesday night I will be over to see you." A whole lot of so-called worship is like that today. It will not take very much to keep us away from God.

In a marriage ceremony there is something I occasionally use. I think how sacred it is. The two being joined in marriage say, "With my body I thee worship."

The hero swam the Hellespont every evening to be with the one he loved. One evening he did not come. She knew something had happened, and the next day she found his lifeless body washed ashore. Oh, my friend, to have a heart that goes out to God in adoration. Gregory Nazianzen said, "I love God because I know Him; I adore Him because I cannot understand Him; I bow before Him in awe and in worship and adoration." Oh, have you found that adoration in your worship?

Then, last of all, there is *exaltation* in worship. And I do not mean the exaltation of God—we put God in His rightful place when we worship Him. When you and I are down on our faces before Him, we are taking the place that the creature should take before the Creator. I am not speaking here of the exaltation of God; rather, I am speaking now of the exaltation of man.

Humanism with its deadening philosophy has been leading man back to the jungle for about half a century, and we are not very far from the jungle. It is degrading to become a lackey, a menial. And think of the millions of people who got their tongues black by licking the boots of Hitler! Humanism did that. They turned their backs on God. And when man turns his back on God, he will worship a man. No atheist, no agnostic, has ever turned his back on God who did not get his tongue black by licking somebody's boots. There is nothing that will exalt man, there is nothing that will give dignity to man, like worshiping God.

Dr. Harry Emerson Fosdick wrote a sermon in the 1920s entitled "The Peril of Worshiping Jesus." In this message he said that men have tried two ways to get rid of Jesus: one by crucifying Him, the other by worshiping Him. The liberal doesn't like you to worship Jesus. My friend, I worship Him. He is my Lord; He is my God. I do not find it humiliating to fall down before Him. There is nothing as exalting and as thrilling as to get down on your face before Jesus Christ. In Acts, chapter 9, the record tells us that Paul fell into the dust of the Damascus Road, and the Lord Jesus dealt with him there. Then notice that He told him to arise—stand up on his feet. Only the Christian faith has ever lifted a man out of the dust and put him on his feet. In the first chapter of Revelation we read that John, on the Isle of Patmos, saw the glorified Christ. John says, "And when I saw him, I fell at his feet as dead. And he laid his right hand upon me, saying unto me, Fear not . . ." (Rev. 1:17). The creature now can come to the Creator. Man, who has been lost in sin, who has gone down and down, can come up and up and worship Christ.

During the seventeenth century Muretus, a great scholar of that day, was going through Lombardy when he suddenly became ill and was picked up on the street. They took him to the hospital, and, thinking he was a bum, the doctors said something like this, "Let's try an experiment on this worthless creature." They were speaking in Latin and had no notion their patient could understand them. But Muretus answered them in Latin, "Will you call one worthless for whom Jesus Christ did not disdain to die?" My friend, it is only Jesus Christ and the worship of Him that has lifted man up.

Man is yet to be restored to his rightful place some day, and brought back into harmony with heaven.

The Great Psalm 150 begins with the Son of God pulling out the stop Diapason: "Praise ye the LORD. Praise God in his sanctuary: praise him in the firmament of his power."

Then the Flute stop is pulled out: "Praise him with the sound of the trumpet: praise him with the psaltery and harp."

Then the String stop is pulled out: "Praise him with the timbrel and dance: praise him with stringed instruments and organs."

Then listen, my beloved: "Let every thing that hath breath praise the LORD." In the beginning God breathed life into man—soul and spirit—but man departed from God. Now there is coming a day when everything that has life, everything that has breath, shall praise the LORD. Even now in this day in which you and I are living we can lift our hearts and lives to Him in adoration and praise.

In my first pastorate, one of my officers thought he was doing me a favor by inviting me to the performance of a symphony orchestra. Now, I know nothing about music, and I do not understand it, but to be nice I went along. I sat there, and I learned something. Before the concert began, one hundred fifty or so musicians came out on the platform. Each one picked up his little instrument and began tuning it. I have never heard such bedlam in my life! Every musician was making his own particular little squeak, regardless of anyone else. Such a medley of noise—it sounded like a boiler factory. Then they all disappeared, and in a few moments they came back out, and the lights went off in the auditorium. It got very quiet. Then the spotlight was focused on the wings, and out stepped the conductor. He came to the podium, turned and bowed. There was great applause. Then it grew quiet again. He lifted the baton—you could have heard a pin drop—then he gave the down beat. My friend, you have never heard such music! Everything was in tune; everything was in harmony.

About me in this world I hear nothing but bedlam. Every man is playing his own little tune. But one of these days out from the wings will step the Conductor, the Lord Jesus Christ. And when He lifts His baton, out yonder at the end of God's universe those galactic systems will burst forth into song. Every bird, every angel, and then man, will join the heavenly chorus.

"Praise ye the LORD. Praise God in his sanctuary: praise him in the firmament of his power. Praise him for his mighty acts: praise him according to his excellent greatness. Praise him with the sound of the trumpet; praise him with the psaltery and harp. Praise him with the timbrel and dance: praise him with stringed instruments and organs. Praise him upon the loud cymbals: praise him upon the high sounding cymbals. Let every thing that hath breath praise the LORD. Praise ye the LORD."

In the meantime, while we are waiting for His return, you and I can bow before Him and bring our little souls into the harmony of heaven.

BIBLIOGRAPHY
(Recommended for Further Study)

Alexander, J. A. *The Psalms*. 1864. Reprint. Grand Rapids, Michigan: Zondervan Publishing House, 1964.

Gaebelein, Arno C. *The Annotated Bible*. 1917. Reprint. Neptune, New Jersey: Loizeaux Brothers, 1970.

Gaebelein, Arno C. *The Book of Psalms*. 1939. Reprint. Neptune, New Jersey: Loizeaux Brothers, 1965. (The finest prophetical interpretation of the Psalms)

Grant, F. W. *The Psalms*. Neptune, New Jersey: Loizeaux Brothers, 1895. (Numerical Bible)

Gray, James M. *Synthetic Bible Studies*. Old Tappan, New Jersey: Fleming H. Revell Co., 1906.

Ironside, H. A. *The Psalms*. Neptune, New Jersey: Loizeaux Brothers, n.d.

Jamieson, Robert; Fausset, A. R.; and Brown, D. *Commentary on the Bible*. 3 vols. Grand Rapids, Michigan: Wm. B. Eerdmans Publishing Co., 1945.

Jensen, Irving L. *The Psalms*. Chicago, Illinois: Moody Press, 1970. (A self-study guide)

Morgan, G. Campbell. *Notes on the Psalms*. Old Tappan, New Jersey: Fleming H. Revell Co., 1947.

Olson, Erling C. *Meditations in the Psalms*. Neptune, New Jersey: Loizeaux Brothers, 1939. (Devotional)

Perowne, J. J. Stewart. *The Book of Psalms*. 1882. Reprint. Grand Rapids, Michigan: Zondervan Publishing House, 1976.

Sauer, Erich. *The Dawn of World Redemption*. Grand Rapids, Michigan; Wm. B. Eerdmans Publishing Co., 1061. (An excellent Old Testament survey)

Scroggie, W. Graham. *The Psalms*. Old Tappan, New Jersey: Fleming H. Revell Co., 1948. (Excellent)

Scroggie, W. Graham. *The Unfolding Drama of Redemption*. Grand Rapids, Michigan: Zondervan Publishing House, 1970. (An excellent survey and outline of the Old Testament)

Spurgeon, Charles Haddon. *The Treasury of David*. 3 vols. Reprint. Grand Rapids, Michigan: Zondervan Publishing House, 1974. (A classic work and very comprehensive)

Unger, Merrill F. *Unger's Bible Handbook*. Chicago, Illinois: Moody Press, 1966. (A basic tool for every Christian's library)

Unger, Merrill F. *Unger's Commentary on the Old Testament*. Vol. 1. Chicago, Illinois: Moody Press, 1981. (A fine summary of each paragraph—Highly recommended)